CONTENT WITH PURPOSE

Authentic Messaging and Marketing to Grow Your Business

SHANNON EMMERSON

The author can be reached as follows: shannon@forgeandspark.com | www. forgeandspark.com

Published by Prominence Publishing.

Content With Purpose/Emmerson, Shannon. -- 1st ed.

ISBN: 978-1-990830-88-4

To Ryan, who reminded me:

"If not you, then who?"

TABLE OF CONTENTS

"Authenticity is the daily practice of letting go of who we think we're supposed to be and embracing who we are."

BRENÉ BROWN

THANKS

I am so very grateful to the following people for encouraging and supporting during the completion of this book: Suzanne Doyle-Ingram and her fabulous cohort of authors, Brent Hopkin, Zac Hopkin, Emma Payne, Ali MacIntyre, Kari Nye, and my mom and dad, Sharon and Bob Emmerson. Special thanks to Lisa Manfield and Mindy Abramowitz for serving as my beta readers and offering their deeply helpful editorial guidance (and emotional support); to Christina Tran for her beautiful work on this book cover; and to Lara Kroeker for her fierce support in growing our agency and in developing my first course on messaging, which led directly to this book. I extend further thanks to my incredible Forge & Spark team for contributing to the approaches, tools, and templates used throughout this book—and for making me so very proud of the work we do in the world.

PREFACE

My early career was driven by a clear purpose: to elevate the efforts of the corporations I worked for. Like a dutiful Gen Xer, I threw myself into serving others. As I moved through various roles in publishing and communications, I did what I was asked. I wrote newsletters hawking magazine subscriptions. I created website banner ads with bold colours and terrible font combinations. I designed microsites and landing pages and crafted copy to lure the reader into doing what my bosses wanted them to do.

I had mastered the art of creating marketing copy and content for other brands, using techniques that delivered results without a whole lot of truth or substance. But when I launched my own content consultancy at 41, I found myself paralyzed by the daunting task of marketing my own business. I didn't want to promote my business using that sales-y language and those shady tactics that absolutely did not reflect who I was as a person or what I stood for as a new brand. But I didn't know how to translate what I did stand for into a business and marketing that I could take pride in.

It took years of working both in and on my business—making a lot of mistakes and celebrating a few sweet wins—before I could talk about my business with real confidence and clarity. And I'll tell you, that shift happened only when I took a step back, redefined my purpose, and realigned my values to feel true to who I am and who I want to serve, instead of trying to be or do what I thought I was supposed to.

I realized that it brought me joy to use my particular set of skills to help the 'good guys' rather than the corporations. I adored supporting non-profits, and leaders with vision launching social impact businesses or striving to become B Corps, and small business owners committed to giving back to their community. I loved dreaming of better things with leaders who cared about helping people—their teams as well as their customers—at least as much as they appreciated profit and business growth.

Over time I recognized that I had the power to choose who I worked with and who I didn't support, and that I could shape my company to reflect my values. I realized that I could run my business on purpose, and that my marketing could, and should, express that.

So I did. I doubled down on what I wanted to do and quit doing what I didn't. I shifted our agency's focus to serving purpose-driven businesses and leaders: people in business dedicated to creating meaningful change—whether through environmental stewardship, supporting their communities, or standing up for what's right. We also joined the B Corp movement, committing ourselves as a business to creating positive impact in line with our deeply-held values.

This shift in my mindset changed my business fundamentally—and it changed the way I talked about it. I stood taller. I spoke with more clarity. I was able to tell my story with an authority I didn't know I had. And that was because it was finally a story I wanted to tell: one rich with people doing good things for one another whose next chapter made me feel curious, inspired, and excited.

Perhaps you've felt something similar—a moment when the good work you're doing aligns with what you believe in, when you see its real impact, and you can't help but feel encouraged, energized, and proud. And when you talk about it, I'll just bet there's a light in your eyes, a spark that other people can't miss.

Content with purpose—authentic communication that cares about connecting with others, rather than just selling to them—is that spark.

It's about communicating your purpose and values and all you do in a way that helps you to grow your business. It comes from living and loving your business: knowing who you serve, and the value you provide based on what your customers truly want and need from you. And it's about creating content and marketing that not only drives your business forward but also resonates with your audience because it's rooted in your unique purpose and values.

The world needs you and what you bring to it. It's my hope that this book inspires and empowers you to share your good work in the world with confidence, clarity, and passion.

"Only connect the prose and the passion, and both will be exalted."

E.M. FORSTER

INTRODUCTION

In the 1970s and 1980s, I sometimes felt like everything I heard was a lie. I learned at one point that subliminal messages were planted in a photograph of ice cubes in a magazine ad. Another ad asked me, "Who told you the earth was warming?" Marketing told me smoking was not only acceptable but super glamorous! Aspartame, I understood, was delicious.

It was a world of shiny, happy people, and we were supposed to pretend that we all felt fine, even when we really, really didn't.

Before I started writing this book, a few problems were jangling around in my head, tangling around one another: finding and living your purpose; figuring out an alternative to all the fake-feeling, trendy reels and short videos that other business leaders were putting out; and coming up with some kind of system that connected what I knew about content marketing with what I was learning about creating a purpose-driven business.

And when, one afternoon during a walk up the hill in my neighbourhood park, I heard these words through my headphones on Audible, I felt like I'd found a missing piece of the puzzle in my brain.

> *"People have two basic needs. Attachment and authenticity. When authenticity threatens attachment ... attachment trumps authenticity."*
>
> —Dr. Gabor Maté, *The Myth of Normal*

Throughout his body of work, Dr. Gabor Maté writes and speaks about the tension between our human drive for attachment—the essential closeness we need for survival—and our need for authenticity, which is about being true to who we are, following our gut, and living in a way that reflects deep self-knowledge.

He observes that children can often get caught in a conflict between their need to connect with and be accepted by their caregivers (attachment) and a growing sense of who they are (authenticity). If (and when) these needs clash, he says, children most frequently choose to sacrifice their authentic selves in favour of acceptance. They hide themselves to please and be accepted by those caregivers. So while their sacrifice serves as a survival mechanism, it's one that can lead to a deep disconnection from their true selves.

As adults, the repercussions of misrepresenting ourselves in a business setting are, of course, nowhere near as dire. We might simply find ourselves blushing at a networking event when we stumble over our elevator pitch, or, worse, not showing up at such events because we don't know what the heck to say when asked that terrifying question: *So, what is it that you do?*

Not knowing how to speak about ourselves as leaders, brands, and businesses, comes from being faced with an infinite variety of responses, and not knowing which to choose. Do you offer up your resume? Do you talk about your latest project or the one you care about most? Do you say what's really on your mind or do you smile and get ready to pitch?

Far too often, business culture has taught us to defer to bluster, and to try to persuade others that we're more successful, more effective, richer, smarter, more competent, that we feel, or are. And it feels bloody awful—both to be the person spreading such messaging, as well as to be its audience.

It struck me on that day in the park that *this* is the conflict between authenticity and attachment. We want to belong, of course. We want our listeners to pay attention. We want to grow our social audiences, and the number or quality of our leads and customers and clients. But we find ourselves continuing to use outmoded messaging, as business leaders, marketers, businesses, and brands.

And when we compromise our authenticity in any context, I think we lose something of incredible value: the opportunity for genuine connection and trust with other people—including our colleagues, teams, partners, customers, and audiences.

Only Connect

Connection is everything. It's the common magic that happens when we 'get' one another—often brought about, by sharing ideas, stories, or moments of understanding.

I'll share a quick story. One evening this past year, I made my way to the second of two networking events. The first that night had been with 'my people': entrepreneurs in the social impact space at a little restaurant in East Vancouver. I'd known several people, and felt at ease even when chatting with people I didn't know. This second event, though, was the other kind—name tags, awkward handshakes, bad lighting, and nobody I knew at all. How had I even signed up for this thing?

I was cursing my own biz dev overzealousness when I found myself in an unexpectedly memorable conversation. This person—someone I'd never met—approached me tentatively and complimented my boots: an old pair of hot pink John Fleuvogs I'd bought more than 20 years prior, and happened to have dug out of my closet that week. This person's shyness, curiosity, and dry humour drew me in, and I found myself recalling my reason for buying the boots (Fleuvog named them 'the Shannons') and telling a story about the last time I'd worn them (to a Ween concert with my brother). It turned out that this person had listened to Ween too, back in the day, and that they were a much bigger Fleuvog fanatic than me. We laughed and talked about hating events like this, and what we really liked instead, for about 15 minutes before we both made our escapes, agreeing to keep in touch (we have).

It was one simple conversation with one person who made me feel seen and known at a time I especially appreciated and needed it. And here I am telling you about it nearly a year later.

In his book *Supercommunicators: How to Unlock the Secret Language of Connection*, Charles Duhigg might call this attuned conversation. Effective conversation, he says, "requires recognizing what kind of conversation is occurring, and then matching each other." That's often the beginning of connection. Further, he notes that "to communicate with someone, we must connect with them. When we absorb what someone is saying and they comprehend what we say, it's because our brains have, to some degree, aligned."

This is something that happens every day in conversations between people. But it's my contention that this can, and should, happen in your business communication and marketing, too.

Compare the Fleuvog conversation to another all-too-familiar networking scenario: someone approaches, asks what you do, and—before you can even finish your answer—their eyes are scanning the room for their next target. They're not listening to you, but rather waiting for their turn to talk, when, rather than seeking out a point of connection, you just know they'll deliver rehearsed lines designed to impress someone that isn't you.

These exchanges are not only disheartening, but maddening to me. They don't just waste our precious time—they waste our potential.

And here's the thing: whether you're chatting over cold hors d'hoeuvres at a networking event or communicating your latest offering in a LinkedIn post, every interaction, and every piece of content, holds the potential to leave someone better than you found them.

Purpose-led businesses are powered by ideas, vision, and passion. The people behind and within these organizations pour their energy into creating products and services that help people or advance causes that matter, and have incredible stories to tell. I suspect that you are one of these people. And I will tell you: it is absolutely possible to use your passions, your interests, your values, and your utterly unique stories not just to connect but to grow. To build trust. And to spark real, meaningful change.

That's what this book is about. It's about showing up as you are, and making your potential moments of connection really count.

The Value of Authentic Content Today

Content marketing is challenging to create and even harder to get right. It's like trying to assemble IKEA's Liatorp wall system without the right instructions—frustrating, confusing, and possibly leading to bouts of weeping. So throwing things like authenticity in the mix might feel overwhelming, or, worse, self-indulgent. Why not, after all, just 'do what's always worked?' To get results in marketing, it's been pretty normal to stretch or 'spin' the facts, twist the truth slightly, and use words and phrases that, while coming off as smarmy, do yield sales or results.

I know. I wrote a lot of that copy. Some of it did "work." It got people to buy things. But a lot of it had 'the ick.' And because I wrote it, I felt I had 'the ick' too. I felt dishonest and manipulative and I no longer wanted that.

And I'm not alone.

Authenticity is essential for building trust, and trust is the foundation of meaningful relationships. So show up as you are and reveal what's real.

Creating content that's rooted in your brand's values and purpose is worth your valuable time and effort. Thoughtful, honest content does take work, and it can be tempting to go for quick, surface-level wins. But in my experience, investing in deeper, more genuine content pays off absolutely.

"To recruit someone, you have to convince them that you care about them, which means you have to actually care about them, which means you have to connect in some way."

CHARLES DUHIGG, SUPERCOMMUNICATORS

Where Authentic Content is Needed Most

High-quality, authentic content marketing is particularly well-suited to businesses like mine (service businesses and agencies that rely on long-term relationships) as well as the following kinds of organizations:

Service-based businesses: Consultants and businesses that depend on building and maintaining trust-based, long-term relationships with clients, can use authentic content to showcase expertise, build credibility, and nurture relationships with potential and current customers over time.

Purpose-driven organizations: Companies with a clear mission or purpose beyond profit can use authentic content to showcase their values and demonstrate their real-world impact, attracting like-minded customers and partners.

Thought leaders and experts: Individuals and brands positioning themselves as authorities in their field might use authentic content to demonstrate expertise, share insights, and build credibility with their audience (plus offer a bit of helpful advice along the way).

B2B businesses with complex sales cycles: Businesses selling high-value products or services can educate prospects, address concerns, and nurture long-term relationships throughout extended decision-making processes—all with the help of high-quality content.

Startups: New businesses seeking an 'in' within established markets can use content to differentiate themselves, articulate their unique value proposition, and develop trust with customers who might be wary of newcomers.

Brands in sensitive industries: Companies in fields like finance, healthcare, or personal services often use content marketing to address concerns, build confidence, and establish the trust necessary for customers to feel comfortable engaging with them.

For these and other types of businesses, thoughtful content that accurately expresses their approach, attitudes, and values, isn't just an effective tactic for achieving marketing goals. Authentic content can also be a powerful tool for building the trust, credibility, and long-term relationships that are important to their growth and success.

How This Book Is Organized

Content With Purpose can serve as a guide to marketing with authenticity and ethical principles. It is designed for leaders and marketers who aspire to create content marketing that not only achieves results but also aligns with their brand identity, core values, and desired impact. In this book, I've provided the tools and framework to develop messaging and content that has the potential to resonate with audiences, foster trust, and express the best qualities of what your brand represents.

At its core, *Content With Purpose* is a guide for people who believe that authenticity should be the cornerstone of leadership and communication. It's for brands and organizations that care about more than just the bottom line—whether you're a B Corp, a social venture, a non-profit, or someone committed to making a positive difference in the work you do. And it's for people who want to sound uniquely like themselves, rather than a pale version of everyone else.

Throughout the book, you'll find practical guidance on how to shape key messages, Story Pillars, and content strategies that truly connect with your audience. If your focus is on short-term sales or viral publicity, there are other resources that might suit you better. *Content With Purpose* is for those ready to lean into who they are, what they stand for, and how to authentically engage their audience.

Here's how we'll move through this together.

First, we dive into strategies and advice specifically tailored for purpose-driven brands, B Corps, social ventures, and not-for-profits. Through real-life examples, you'll see how to use content marketing to express your values and mission and achieve tangible results. This book is about helping you create content that aligns with your purpose so you can connect meaningfully with those who matter most.

Next, we'll explore an actionable framework for building your unique Messaging Map. This map is based on your organization's purpose, values, and mission, guiding you in what to say and how to say it at every stage of your content journey. With clarity and intention, you'll learn how to craft messages that resonate deeply with your audience, making your marketing more effective and authentic.

Finally, this book touches on how to apply the messaging you've developed to the day-to-day and month-to-month content and communications you use in your business. You'll receive guidance on using your foundational messaging to identify the Story Pillars, themes, and formats that will give shape to the stories you most need to tell.

Creating content and communications that feels truly authentic to you and your brand is a journey that takes time, but the outcomes—genuine connections, deeper trust, and a brand that reflects your values—are well worth it.

How To Read This Book

Whether you're here to develop your messaging or just seeking an overview of authentic messaging practices, *Content With Purpose* is designed to meet you where you are.

If you aim to craft or refine your messaging, I recommend diving into the book from start to finish. The early chapters lay the groundwork by exploring the 'Why' of purpose—the rise of purpose-driven organizations and the shifts in consumer behaviour that highlight the growing importance of authenticity and genuine connection. Understanding these trends will help you see why your messaging matters so much in today's landscape.

As you move forward, you'll discover where purpose and values fit into modern organizations (spoiler: they belong at the very foundation) and how your content marketing can evolve from these core principles. You'll learn how to align your business strategy with marketing practices that express integrity and intention, setting the stage for everything that follows.

Later in the book, I'll dig into the nitty-gritty of messaging. Here, you'll find a structured framework you can use—maybe even today—to start outlining clear, connective messages that will guide you and your team across all your sales and marketing efforts, from your website to your content and social media marketing. This part of the book is hands-on and practical, designed to help you show up with messaging that feels right and authentically represents who you are.

On the other hand, if you're looking for an overview of authentic messaging practices—whether for inspiration, insight, or to inform your broader strategy—you might prefer to skim through the earlier sections, focusing on the chapters that resonate most with your current needs. The book is packed with examples and principles you can apply in your work, even if you're not ready to roll up your sleeves and dive into the entire framework.

However you choose to read *Content With Purpose*, I hope it leaves you with a deeper understanding of how to create messaging that's true to your values and effective in connecting with your audience. Whether you're here for a comprehensive guide or a high-level overview, this book is your companion in building marketing that matters.

"Find out
who you are
and do it
on purpose."

DOLLY PARTON

CHAPTER 1

WHAT IS MESSAGING
(AND WHAT'S *YOURS* SAYING)?

When I was growing up in the 80s and 90s, marketing and advertising didn't sound natural or human. So much of it sounded terribly fake and salesy. It sounds like the Simpsons character Troy McClure or Ted Baxter from the Mary Tyler Moore show: pompous and puffed up with false authority and bravado, like someone whose opinions you'd be insane not to question.

So, what should your marketing voice sound like?

It should sound like you.

You don't need to put on a fake front, lie, or make false claims in your marketing—these tactics will not serve you well.

People (and let's remember that those faceless-seeming "marketing audiences" are, in fact, a collection of individual humans with unique wishes, intentions, dreams, fears, wants, and needs) have become increasingly skeptical about marketing messages. We're bombarded with ads, promotions, and social content from brands. So, we've become discerning, to say the least, and able to quickly and effectively evaluate the truth and value of most marketing claims.

And because so many of us—who are ourselves nameless, faceless marketing audiences—are skeptical, tired of being lied to and patronized, and rather sick of the sales bullshit, we are speaking up about wanting more transparency and credibility from the brands trying to reach and sell to us.

Our growing skepticism as consumers is undoubtedly a challenge for marketers, but it's also an exciting opportunity.

We now simply need to be better marketers and business leaders. We need to create better content that tells compelling stories, offers evidence-backed claims, and reflects who we truly are.

By showing up authentically—with generosity, intelligence, and empathy—we have the chance to connect with our audience in a meaningful way and win their trust and loyalty.

Audiences want trust.

Trust is no longer a nice-to-have. I see it as the foundation of every meaningful relationship between a brand and its audience. According to the 2023 Edelman Trust Barometer, business has now taken the lead as the most trusted global institution, outpacing both government and media. In a time when trust in traditional institutions is eroding, people are looking to businesses for products and leadership on pressing issues like climate change and economic inequality. They expect brands to act with integrity, to be transparent, and to stand for something real and meaningful. (Source: Edelman[1], Edelman[2]).

Yet, there's a trust gap that's impossible to ignore. The 2023 Havas Meaningful Brands Study shows that only 47% of brands are seen as trustworthy. The situation is even worse in North America, where only 39% of brands earn that trust. In East Asia, the figure drops to a startling 24%. Consumers are skeptical, and they're right to be. We live in an age where distrust has become the default emotion, making it increasingly difficult for brands to connect genuinely (Source: Trust Signals Marketing3).

And it's not just about what you sell. Standing behind this (ideally with pride) is who you are and what you stand for. People care deeply about values and will want to understand yours. The Edelman report found that 71% of consumers say trusting the brands they buy from is more important than ever before. Meanwhile, data from the NYU Stern Center for Sustainable Business shows that sustainability-marketed products are growing twice as fast as conventional ones. Consumers are actively choosing to support brands that align with their values, even if it means paying a wee bit more (Source: Edelman4, Mercer Island Group5)

But here's the kicker: Many brands still fall short despite this apparent demand for integrity and transparency. The Havas study found that 75% of brands could disappear tomorrow, and most people wouldn't bat an eye. That's a glaring sign that brands are over-promising and under-delivering, wouldn't you say? People are losing faith, and the message is clear: We must do better or risk becoming irrelevant. (Source: Trust Signals Marketing6)

So, where does that leave us? It's simple: We need to step up.

We need to be honest in our communications, take responsibility for our actions, and ensure that what we're putting out into the world is not only true but true to who we are. It's time to build trust not just with words but with actions.

The Power of Authenticity in Marketing

So, what is authenticity? For me, it's about aligning our actions, words, and values. It's a fundamental part of living and leading with purpose.

In life, being authentic means honoring our values, acting in ways that reflect who we truly are, and having the courage to show up without feeling pressured to conform. Psychology tells us that living in this way can deepen relationships and enhance well-being. And when we're true to ourselves, we naturally invite others to connect with us on a more meaningful level.

In work, authenticity goes a step further by creating an environment where people feel safe, trusted, and engaged. Leaders who stay true to their values inspire teams, fostering a culture of openness and productivity. When people summon up the courage to show up as their genuine selves (and for many, it does require courage), workplaces might just become spaces where people connect and grow.

In marketing, authenticity is the foundation of trust between the brand and audience. It's about presenting a brand truthfully, making sure that every message reflects its real values and commitments. Authentic marketing isn't about catchy slogans or superficial promises; it's about telling stories that genuinely align with a brand's mission and purpose. People are drawn to brands and people that show up with honesty and integrity, and they gravitate toward those that reflect values they believe in.

So why does this matter? At all of these levels—life, work, and communication—authenticity is essential for building trust, fostering connections, and creating real impact. And particularly for purpose-driven brands like B Corps, social ventures, and other mission-oriented organizations, authenticity is essential. It means having a voice that's uniquely yours and ensuring that every message resonates with truth and integrity. This kind of authenticity builds connections that go beyond transactions, creating lasting relationships based on genuine trust and mutual respect. Embracing authenticity is not only a way to lead with purpose but also a way to create content that makes a real, positive impact.

Trustworthy Messaging in Your Marketing

People use the term 'messaging' in oodles of different ways. In this book, I'm looking at messaging as the 'what you need to say' piece in the marketing puzzle, with a good deal of understanding about why you need to say it.

In essence, your marketing messaging is how you communicate—using stories, visuals, content, ads, etc. —your unique value to your audience with resonance, helping you stand out from your competitors.

Your messaging is your way of defining, creating, and communicating key messages about your brand that will best capture and express what you determine is most important for your audience to know AND what they want to know about your brand.

It involves two key things to create resonance: what you want (and feel you need) to say and what they want to know.

Resonance: Achieving the Elusive Message-Market Match

Message-market match is all about aligning your messaging with what your audience needs and cares about. When you achieve this alignment, your content doesn't just reach your audience, it resonates with them. Considering your audience's needs takes you out of your own head, as it were, and requires that you consider what's in your audience's head and heart. It's where strategy meets empathy.

Far too often, I've seen brands default to inward-focused marketing, prioritizing their product features and achievements over their audience's needs and/or desires. They express only what they care about and lose their audience's attention and interest entirely. A software company might, for example, highlight its latest features without addressing how these solve user problems. A consulting firm might emphasize how it differs from competitors without considering whether potential customers recognize those competitors as relevant to them. This inward approach can lead to content and campaigns that miss the mark, leaving audiences feeling disconnected and undervalued, ultimately damaging the brand's credibility and trustworthiness.

So, how do you avoid this? It starts with understanding your audience—both their emotional and practical needs. This means knowing who you want to reach and digging deep into their challenges. What are they struggling with? What outcomes do they most desire? Your messaging should bridge these gaps, providing clear solutions that speak directly to their needs.

What you know
and **need to say**

Message-
Market Match

What your audience
needs from you

What It Takes

Achieving a solid message-market match requires that you understand your audience and their emotional and practical needs. You need to understand the topics they're interested in, the questions they have, what they're struggling with, and what they most want the outcome to be.

Of course, the first thing is knowing who you are most interested in reaching and engaging—identifying your most important audiences. The next bit is understanding those audiences: considering your audience's main problem or challenge in the context of what you're marketing and exactly how your content can provide a solution.

This process requires research and a deep understanding of the various channels through which you will deliver your message (e.g., social media, website, email, etc.).

Only when you understand your target market and the topics that interest them can you effectively craft content that meets their interests and, with practice, serves your business, too.

We'll explore how to craft your message-market match in more detail later in the book, but for now, keep this concept in mind as you start thinking about the kinds of messaging you want to create. Whether it's broad brand messaging that defines who you are or more specific product/service messaging that drives action, the key is to ensure it all resonates with the people you're trying to reach.

Brand Messaging Vs. Product/Service Messaging

So, what *are* the key messages you'll need to communicate? Well, on a broad level, you probably want to share what you do, how you do it, and why it should matter to your customers or audiences. You may want to highlight the values that guide you, enabling your audiences to quickly understand what you're all about. On a more tactical level, you'll also want messaging that helps you make that sale, persuade your customer to take some kind of action, and give your audience all the information and rationale they need to decide about your product or service.

The easiest way to divide this high-level vs. tactical messaging is to consider your Brand Messaging first and then your more specific Product or Service Messaging.

Brand Messaging speaks, of course, about your brand. It's your 'umbrella messaging' that the rest of your messaging, marketing copy, and campaigns live under. It encapsulates your brand identity and values and should help you connect with people on an emotional level.

Product and Service Messaging, on the other hand, is tactical and specific. It should inform and drive action. Informed by your overall brand messaging, this kind of messaging will persuasively capture the benefits or features of your products and services.

Brand Messaging: Your Top 5

Your brand messaging should capture your purpose, your values, and your brand's uniqueness. It should capture what you stand for and offer to the world.

Great brand messaging will succinctly convey who and what you are and how you're different from your competitors (and who they are) while emotionally resonating with your audience.

It involves crafting messages that reflect your brand's purpose, values, and personality so that all your product and service messaging (and indeed every piece of content your brand creates) resonates with your target audiences, reinforcing your brand reputation and the promises you've made.

Below is a brief summary of what I consider the critical types of messaging to create for your brand.

1. Your Core Brand Message

A core brand message is a concise statement that communicates the essence of your brand to its audience. It should efficiently encapsulate the central idea or value that a brand wants to convey to its customers and stakeholders while acknowledging why that should matter to the audience. It's the first and perhaps most important example of where that message-market match comes into play, answering these two key questions:

- What does the brand offer?

- Why does it matter to the audience?

This message should be unique, memorable, and relevant to the brand's identity and purpose. Nike's iconic "Just do it" is an excellent example, encapsulating the brand's ethos of determination and motivation, and the part its products play in enabling people to push their limits regardless of challenges. This message should also be true wherever an audience encounters it, so it needs to be consistent across all marketing channels and touchpoints to create a strong brand image and build brand loyalty. The core brand message is an essential component of a brand's overall marketing strategy and helps to differentiate it from its competitors. That's a tall order, right? Don't fret. We'll walk you through defining yours.

2. Your Brand's Unique Value Proposition

Also known as your UVP, this is the ingredient that makes you what you are. (Note that you may likely also want to create UVP statements for specific products / services, as described below.) I'm going to cite the definition provided by April Dunford, author of *Obviously Awesome: How to Nail Product Positioning So Customers Get It, Buy It, Love It*, here:

> "Your value proposition is the unique combination of benefits you offer to customers. It's the reason customers buy from you instead of your competitors. A great value proposition is a clear statement that explains how your product solves customers' problems or improves their situation, delivers specific benefits, and tells the ideal customer why they should buy from you and not from the competition."

A brilliant example already cited in this book is Patagonia's "We're in business to save our home planet." Many companies have to do a lot of work to define their UVP. You might, too, and I'll give you a starting point in this book.

3. Your Brand Purpose / Mission Statement

Knowing what drives you as a brand (beyond making a profit) is foundational. And if it's important and authentic to you, it may well be worth communicating. I'm not a huge fan of the traditional corporate Mission Statement of the 'we do X so that Y' variety, preferring to inject a bit of real purpose into the mix. This statement should get to the heart of your brand's overarching purpose or mission, including the impact you strive to create through what you do. A good purpose statement will enable your audience to get what you're about instantly and will serve as a guide for your daily operations and decision-making, ensuring that what you do aligns with your purpose.

I like to use these clear statements from TenTree as an example of purpose messaging: "Earth-First essentials. Planting trees with every purchase."

4. Your Vision Statement

I *always* get purpose/mission statements mixed up with vision statements. Roll them into one if you want. But traditionally, while the Purpose / Mission Statement is focused on the present state, the Vision Statement sets a course for the future. Your Vision Statement should guide your long-term strategy and planning, paving the way for your company's evolution.

And it need not sound grandiose and overblown (as so many corporate vision statements tend to do). Etsy's inspiring but simple vision statement, "Keep commerce human" is an excellent guiding example.

5. Your Core Values

Brand values get at the heart of who you are as a brand and what guides and shapes your decision-making, internal behaviour, and culture as an organization. And most people want to know what you stand for before making a purchase decision. Proud of how you behave? Values will likely be a key feature of your messaging.

I love the way Lush Cosmetics has shared its values in its marketing in a factual and humble way: "We believe in making effective products from fresh organic fruit and vegetables, the finest essential oils and safe synthetics."

Other Kinds of Brand Messaging

In this book, we'll be focusing on crafting the above statements for your business. But it's worth pointing out that you'll likely want to investigate other critical kinds of messaging down the road, including Visual Identity, Positioning, and Voice and Tone.

Product / Service Messaging: Your Top 5

Unlike your overarching Brand Messaging, messaging about your products or services should, ideally, emphasize the unique benefits, features, and value that your offerings bring to your customers. It should clearly outline what your product or service does, how it's different and hopefully better than the competition, and why your audience needs and should want it.

To be effective, your Product/Service Messaging should concisely convey the advantages of your offering, how it solves customer problems, and why it must be their preferred choice. Really good Product/Service Messaging clearly communicates the unique value, benefits, and proof of effectiveness of your product or service, ensuring that every piece of content resonates with your target audience and reinforces your brand's credibility and value proposition.

Here are the five kinds of Product/Service Messages I recommend creating:

1. The Value Proposition Message for Your Product / Service

A value proposition message that's specific to your product/service communicates your product or service's benefits and value to its audience. It should clearly state what makes your product/service unique, the specific problems it solves, and the key benefits it provides. This message should be compelling, differentiating your offering from competitors and addressing why it matters to your audience.

A great product-specific example comes from Who Gives a Crap, a company that makes eco-friendly toilet paper. Their value proposition for toilet paper is simply: "Good for your bum. Great for the world. 50% of our profits are donated to help build toilets for those in need." It's compelling (especially to consumers concerned about sustainability), it's already clear what the product does, and it differentiates their toilet paper from other brands that don't focus on social impact. Rather good, all in all.

2. Benefit Messaging

A benefit-oriented message highlights the specific benefits and positive outcomes that users will experience from your product or service. It focuses on how your offering improves the user's life or business, emphasizing real, tangible benefits. This message should be clear and impactful, showcasing your product/service's value and advantages.

An example: "With every purchase, TOMS will give a new pair of shoes to a child in need. One for One." This messaging from TOMS states the benefit to customers: by buying shoes, they're directly helping children in need.

3. Feature Messaging

A feature message details the key features and functionalities of your product or service. It describes the main features in a way that demonstrates how they contribute to the overall value and benefits. This message should be informative and concise, helping your audience understand the unique aspects of your offering.

Product-specific feature messaging can be seen in product marketing for Seventh Generation (a B Corp) laundry detergent: "Our Free & Clear Laundry Detergent is powered by plant-based ingredients and is 96% USDA Certified Biobased. This hypoallergenic formula is free from dyes, fragrances, and artificial brighteners, making it gentle on sensitive skin. Our innovative triple-enzyme technology tackles tough stains while being safe for septic systems and greywater use." The example illustrates how Seventh Generation describes their product features while also highlighting the product's sustainability and social impact, which are valued by and beneficial to their target audience.

4. Proof Messaging

A proof/validation message builds trust and credibility by providing evidence that supports your claims. It includes testimonials, case studies, endorsements, and statistics that demonstrate the effectiveness and satisfaction of your product or service. This message should be compelling and credible, reinforcing the reliability and value of your offering.

A great example of proof messaging can be seen in nearly every B Corp's proud claim to certification. B Corp certification serves as proof for companies like Patagonia, Tentree, and our own, validating the company's commitment to social and environmental responsibility.

5. Call to Action (CTA) Messaging

What action do you most need your audience to take after seeing your content or communications? A call to action message will guide your audience to take a specific action, such as making a purchase, signing up for a newsletter, or perhaps booking a call or asking for a demo. This kind of messaging should be remarkably clear, concise, and compelling, telling your audience exactly what to do next. This message will be strategically placed on your website and/or within your content or advertising, so it must be easy to understand and motivate your audience to engage with your product or service.

A simple example? MEC's call to "Become a member." This CTA encourages customers to join MEC's co-operative model, fostering a sense of community and shared values.

An Aspirational Example of Purpose: Patagonia

Possibly the best-known example of a purpose-driven company with exceptional marketing is Patagonia. Patagonia grabbed business headlines in 2022, after nearly 50 years in business, for effectively giving $100 million per year in company profits to the earth. The Chouinard family, who previously owned the outdoor clothing and gear company, transferred their ownership of Patagonia to two new entities they created: the Patagonia Purpose Trust and the Holdfast Collective, organizations existing for the purpose of making company profits available to fight climate change. Furthermore, the company announced that any money that is not reinvested back into Patagonia will be distributed as dividends to protect the plan

This is jaw-dropping stuff. A press release from the company on September 14, 2022 described the transition as "'going purpose' instead of 'going public,'" the intention being to "ensure that there is never deviation from the intent of the founder and to facilitate what the company continues to do best: demonstrate as a for-profit business that capitalism can work for the planet."

Yvon Chouinard, Patagonia's founder who remains a board member, explained the move this way:

> *"It's been a half-century since we began our experiment in responsible business. If we have any hope of a thriving planet 50 years from now, it demands all of us doing all we can with the resources we have. As the business leader I never wanted to be, I am doing my part. Instead of extracting value from nature and transforming it into wealth, we are using the wealth Patagonia creates to protect the source. We're making Earth our only shareholder. I am dead serious about saving this planet."*

How's that for setting the 'business as a force for good' bar? And for making the brand the story? Let's take a look at how this impressive company has developed and applied its messaging.

Purpose Reflected in Company Values and Storytelling

But even before this historic decision, Patagonia was arguably one of the world's best-known examples of a purpose-driven company.

On the eve of its 50th anniversary in 2022, the company regrouped to determine how it would approach its next 50 years. They made a few BIG decisions, as you've just learned, INCLUDING remaining a B Corp and continuing to give one percent of sales each year to grassroots activists. But also on the agenda was updating its core values "to reflect the company we want to be as we embark on the next 50 years." Among those values were quality, integrity, environmentalism, justice, and not being bound by convention. Traditional values, you might think (perhaps with the exception of the last). But it's their definition of each that marks their difference in thinking and approach.

In defining quality, for example, Patagonia practically sets out a vision statement for this core value: "Build the best product, provide the best service, and constantly improve everything we do. The best product is useful, versatile, long-lasting, repairable, and recyclable. Our ideal is to make products that give back to the Earth as much as they take." Now that's a clearly stated, actionable, and measurable value.

Their others are in keeping. Within the value of integrity is this statement: "Examine our practices openly and honestly, learn from our mistakes, and meet our commitments." Describing justice, they say: "We aspire to be a company where people from all backgrounds, identities, and experiences have the power to contribute and lead." Environmentalism: "Protect our home planet. We're all part of nature, and every decision we make is in the context of the environmental crisis challenging humanity."

As for their value of being "not bound by convention," their definition is simply this: "Do it our way. Our success—and much of the fun—lies in developing new ways to do things."

Patagonia's values messaging is everywhere: rooted in quality, environmentalism, integrity, and justice, the company frequently shares content and advertising highlighting the quality of their products, the integrity and transparency of their operations, exactly what they're doing to help our 'home planet', their commitments to justice, and their efforts to constantly innovate and 'buck' convention.

The company's messaging, in general, highlights their use of sustainable materials, their environmentalism and support for environmental causes, and their efforts to reduce their own carbon footprint, along with prominent programs that demonstrate their 'walking the walk' in terms of protecting the planet.

And in analyzing Patagonia's marketing, it becomes clear that their core brand message is about Patagonia's commitment to environmental sustainability and activism, and its ethical business practices.

They use their Purpose/Mission/Vision statement frequently in their marketing, too ("We're in business to save our home planet")—offering up a very good argument for making our own messaging this memorable, succinct, and aspirational.

The Impact of Purpose-Led Marketing and Messaging

A 2021 study on the reputation of corporations7 in the U.S. placed Patagonia in first place, with an index score of 82.7, based on consumer perception of the brand. The company is frequently cited as a model for a company that can both live its purpose and achieve business success, as it should be. I would also argue that it's a brilliant example of a brand with crystal-clear messaging and powerful storytelling and that this has unarguably been a factor in its success.

Today, the company proudly supports grassroots causes with its corporate—and marketing—might. The Patagonia Action Works8 program, for example, links people visiting their website with environmental groups in their local area, encouraging them to get involved and take action, whether through volunteering, donations, events, or signing petitions.

They're well-versed in taking public action and managing public relations, too. Again, in 2018, Patagonia sued9 the Trump Administration, objecting to its plan to reduce the size of two national monuments in Utah, generating significant press coverage and public attention. And in 2021, it donated US$1 million10 to fight restrictive voting laws in Georgia.

Patagonia is also well-known for its unconventional marketing. In the 2011 Black Friday edition of the New York Times, Patagonia published a full-page ad11 that specifically advised readers to not buy their clothing. Their "Don't Buy This Jacket" ad outlined all the reasons that consumers shouldn't buy the jacket shown in the image, including:

In the 2011 Black Friday edition of the New York Times, Patagonia published a full-page ad12 that specifically advised readers to not buy their clothing. Their "Don't Buy This Jacket" ad outlined all the reasons that consumers shouldn't buy the jacket shown in the image, including:

- The costs at each stage of manufacturing and making the jacket available

- The need for 135 litres of water to make the jacket (enough water for 45 people)

- The generation of 20 pounds of Co2 by transportation to get the jacket to consumers

But the ad's real message? Buy only what you need, only when you need it. The ad clearly underlines the quality and thought that goes into Patagonia's products, illustrating that they are ethically made and made to last. In other words, *if you're going to buy a jacket you need, this is it.*

The outcome of the campaign: a **30%** rise in sales!

A few years later, in 2015, the brand launched what it called a Worn Wear Wagon: a mobile repair shop that travelled through the US fixing consumer's Patagonia (and sometimes other) clothing and gear, and teaching people how to do it themselves, too. Today, Patagonia customers who bring their old items into a store or who sell them on the website are given credits towards their next purchase of either a new or used Patagonia product. The underlying messages: *we live our values* and *we stand by our stuff.*

It's damned good marketing, good business, and good for the planet, too.

These examples illustrate the depth of Patagonia's commitment to social and environmental causes. I think they also show that while growth and profit have never been the only goal for the company, their clear purpose, willingness to act on it, and powerful storytelling—which has differentiated them profoundly from competitors—has helped them to grow and thrive, contributing to their wider community.

"A company needs to be profitable in order to stay in business and accomplish all its other goals—not for profit itself."

—YVON CHOUINARD

Other Examples of Effective Purpose-Rooted Messaging and Marketing

We aren't all Patagonia. Nor should we be; we're properly busy being our unique and amazing business selves. But we might learn from their example in how to effectively reflect our own values in our marketing while doing some social good, too.

Check out these well-known purpose statements and take a few minutes to guess which brand is behind each.

- To inspire and nurture the human spirit—one cup and one neighbourhood at a time
- To make a positive experience of beauty accessible to every woman
- To bring the best user experience to customers through innovative hardware, software, and services
- To accelerate the world's transition to sustainable energy

My bet is that you got at least one or two. Starbucks, Dove, Apple, and Tesla sometimes say these things in their marketing, but most often, they come out as a story, or series of stories, told through actions as well as their brand communications and marketing. Below you'll find a few other examples of how purpose-led companies use and apply their messaging.

Help Texts

Help Texts is a Seattle-based software company delivers a full year of personalized support to people facing grief, burnout, caregiving and more. At a time when getting affordable, expert help when someone dies is nearly impossible, Help Texts is helping people in 44 countries and all 50 US states to find hope and meaning, even in the darkest of times. The brand is about making sure nobody feels alone when life is as hard as it can get.

Help Texts' purpose is evident in every text they send and every post they publish. Focusing on delivering practical, evidence-based tips and resources, the brand positions itself as a compassionate companion to those in need. While other grief support options - like counseling or attending a support group - can feel daunting and public, Help Texts is easy, immediate and discreet, and has a whopping 95% acceptability rate from grieving people around the world.

Messaging That Resonates on a Personal Level

Help Texts exemplifies a brand that leverages impactful messaging to deeply connect with its audience. Their messaging strategy acknowledges the universal need for support in tough times. Its tagline, "When life gets hard, getting support doesn't have to be," succinctly communicates its mission to provide an easily accessible helping hand. This message not only underlines the service's convenience but also its deep comprehension of its users' emotional needs.

Empathy-Driven Content

Help Texts content is crafted to strike a chord with those in search of comfort and guidance. It balances the universality of grief with the deeply personal and individual experience we all have when someone close to us dies. Through knowledgeable, warm, and open messaging, the brand validates the experience of grief and hardship, offering a ray of hope and actionable support. This empathetic communication ensures that the content is caring and relatable but also practical and helpful at a time when many people feel alone.

Speaking about Help Texts without mentioning the company's founder, Emma Payne, is impossible. Emma founded the company with a deep sense of purpose. After losing her husband to suicide, she experienced what many grievers do, especially after a sudden or traumatic loss. She experienced the deep isolation that comes when friends and family don't know what to say. With 20 years' experience building web and mobile applications already under her belt, Emma founded Help Texts to help people who are grieving, and also to help friends and family who want to help, but don't know how.

Emma has shared her insights on the brand's marketing and messaging approach:

> "At the heart of Help Texts is the belief that everyone deserves to feel supported, especially in their darkest times. Our messaging isn't just about offering a service; it's about offering hope and understanding."

> "We've seen firsthand the power of words when it comes to healing. That's why every message we craft is infused with care and intent, mirroring the compassion we feel for our users."

> "I've been picky about what we say and how/when/where we say it. For example, my team knows that we don't market ourselves in the wake of a celebrity death or national tragedy. Instead we share useful, educational tips and support for how we can all be there for each other when things go pear-shaped. For me it's about genuinely supporting people and being part of the community we serve."

> "All day, every day, beautiful feedback streams into our subscriber support portal. People in the depths of grief take the time to let us know that we are helping them to see the light, honour their loved ones and find hope. That is our brand. That is our messaging approach. Our subscribers tell us how they feel, and their words infuse everything we do. It's not just about testimonials. It's about finding what's at the very heart of our subscribers' experience and sharing that with others looking for light at the end of the tunnel."

Emma's words capture the spirit of Help Texts. This isn't just a business for her; it's a mission, and part of a bigger movement too. Emma has taken a painful experience and committed her business to making a real difference in people's lives through thoughtful, intelligent, and deeply compassionate communication.

Lululemon

Lululemon was born in Vancouver but is now a global manufacturer of athletic and other clothing, best known for its yoga pants. Today, the company is a titan in the athletic apparel industry, and it has seamlessly integrated its core values and purpose into its brand messaging and marketing strategies. Renowned for high-quality yoga and fitness wear, Lululemon has grown a devoted global community by championing and celebrating mindfulness, wellness, and an active lifestyle.

Approach to Messaging and Marketing

Lululemon's marketing transcends the traditional boundaries of selling products, venturing into the realm of promoting a lifestyle that aligns with the company's ethos. The brand's messaging is infused with its commitment to enhancing people's lives through the joy of movement, mindfulness, and community connection.

Key Strategies

- **Community-Centric Initiatives:** Lululemon places huge emphasis on building and nurturing its community. From offering free yoga classes in their stores to organizing local events, they have gone to great lengths to foster a sense of belonging and togetherness among their customers

- **Empowering Brand Ambassadors:** The company's ambassador program enlists yoga instructors, athletes, and influencers who embody Lululemon's values, further amplifying its message through authentic, relatable voices.

- **Purpose-Driven Campaigns:** Lululemon's campaigns often highlight personal transformation stories, celebrating the journey towards wellness and self-discovery. These narratives resonate deeply with their audience, reinforcing the brand's message of personal growth and community support.

Where Lululemon Kicks Butt

- **Authenticity in Communication:** Lululemon's marketing truly feels genuine because—other than employing talented writers and communicators—it's all grounded in the brand's core values of health, mindfulness, and living a life of purpose. It *feels* real. And this authenticity attracts customers who share these values, creating a loyal brand following.

- **Seamless Integration of Purpose and Product:** Unlike brands that seem to tack on purpose as an afterthought, Lululemon's products are designed with its mission in mind. Whether it's through sustainably sourced materials or designs that support the best performance in yoga and fitness, the brand's commitment to its purpose is evident in every product.

- **Engaging Digital Presence:** Through its social media platforms and website, Lululemon shares content that inspires and engages its community. From workout videos and wellness tips to stories of personal transformation, the brand consistently provides value beyond just selling products.

Lululemon's evolution to becoming a top global brand owes much to the company's clearly defined purpose and ridiculously effective marketing. Embodying its core principles and mission in all aspects of its communication has helped Lululemon to differentiate itself within the extremely competitive realm of athletic apparel. Its' steady adherence to founding values—clearly shared by its customers—has helped build a dedicated community of fans who buy into Lululemon's message of staying active and mindful. This example shows how marketing that's driven by a clear purpose can really connect with people, earning their loyalty and pushing the brand and business to success, too.

Genus Capital Management

Genus Capital Management is a wealth management firm walking a line between supporting clients concerned with sensibly managing and ideally growing their wealth and cultivating a new kind of investing—

one that focuses on impact and sustainability. Our agency has worked with Genus (also a certified B Corp in Canada) since 2019, providing strategy and content, so forgive me as I toot our own horn.

Recognized for its innovative approach to wealth management, Genus has distinguished itself by weaving its core mission of sustainable investing into the fabric of its brand identity. This commitment to environmental, social, and governance (ESG) principles has not only set Genus apart but has also cultivated a dedicated community of clients who share their vision for a more responsible approach to investing.

Their messaging is factual, evidence-based, professional, and clear. They try to prompt audiences to rethink traditional attitudes about investing without being pushy or aggressive.

Approach to Messaging and Marketing

Genus's marketing strategy transcends the conventional finance talk, stepping into the realm of advocating for a future where investment goes hand in hand with positive global impact. The company's messaging is steeped in its dedication to driving change through responsible investment practices, highlighting its unique approach in a sector often criticized for lacking sustainability.

Key Strategies

- **Community-Centric Initiatives:** Genus emphasizes creating a network of informed and engaged investors. Through educational workshops, webinars, and sustainability reports, they provide valuable insights, fostering a community united by shared values of responsible investing.

- **Empowering Expert Voices While Showing up as Wholly Human:** By featuring their team of financial experts who specialize in ESG investing, Genus amplifies its message through authoritative, trustworthy sources. These professionals not only represent the brand's values but also serve as advocates for sustainable investing within the broader finance community. They regularly showcase these experts in social media content and webinars, speaking warmly, as well as expertly, in plain language, about key subject areas.

- **Purpose-Driven Campaigns:** Genus shares stories of impact, illustrating the tangible benefits of investing not just on portfolios but on societal and environmental outcomes. These narratives deeply resonate with their audience, underlining Genus's message of financial growth aligned with personal and global well-being.

Where Genus Shines

- **Genuine Commitment:** Genus's marketing is compelling because it's deeply rooted in a genuine commitment to sustainability and ethical investment. This authenticity draws in clients who seek not just financial returns but also to contribute positively to the world.

- **Alignment of Purpose and Service:** Unlike firms that might superficially adopt sustainable practices, Genus's services are built around their mission from the ground up. From ESG-focused portfolios to impact investing, every offering demonstrates their commitment to the values they espouse.

- **Educational Engagement:** Through their digital platforms, Genus doesn't just sell services; they educate and engage. With content that demystifies ESG investing and showcases the impact of sustainable practices, Genus provides value that extends beyond financial advice.

Genus' success as a leader in purpose-based investing showcases the power of aligning brand messaging and marketing with a clear and impactful mission. By embodying its core values of sustainability and responsibility in every communication, Genus has not only differentiated itself in the competitive field of wealth management but has also fostered a community of investors passionate about making a difference. Their example clearly shows how purpose-driven marketing can profoundly connect with clients, earning their trust and propelling a brand towards success.

Tentree

Tentree is another certified B Corp that sells sustainably made clothing to those concerned with fashion, comfort, and reducing the fashion industry's impact on the world. They're known for their commitment to sustainability, reforestation efforts, and ethical manufacturing practices and publicly aim to inspire a global movement towards environmental and social responsibility.

Beyond just selling clothing, TenTree's purpose is to drive positive change and create a lasting impact on the planet. Their messaging is conversational, comfortable, and gently firm about the importance of sustainability in fashion. I love that the brand speaks loudly and plainly about its mission to plant ten trees for every item purchased. This alone highlights something that delivers value to the audience (they can make a positive impact by choosing TenTree) as they speak about the many features of the brand's products customers can choose from.

MEC

MEC, formerly known as Mountain Equipment Co-op, is a Canadian retail cooperative (meaning that it is owned and/or operated by its customers or members) that specializes in outdoor recreational gear and clothing, such as togs for hiking and climbing sets. Its brand purpose is focused on inspiring and enabling people to lead active outdoor lifestyles, and they do that by providing high-quality gear and clothing for outdoor activities like hiking, camping, cycling, and climbing.

Positioning-wise, they celebrate outdoor exploration, urging folks to get out and into nature—in part because it provides the opportunity for personal growth and discovery. Adventure, discovery, and personal growth are hallmark topics in their messaging, which focuses largely on sustainability, engaging their community, and highlighting the brand's outdoor expertise. Given that companies like MEC are up against some tough marketing competition with companies like Patagonia, who are very competitive in terms of quality and sustainability, I would suggest that it's MEC's messaging focus on personal growth and discovery in the context of the outdoors that is the key differentiator in their content.

This kind of messaging shows up in the company's web copy and social media posts like this one, with an image of a couple of hikers scaling a snowy mountaintop. The caption reads:

"At MEC, we're not just about selling gear—we're about living the adventure. When you're an employee at a company, it can be extra challenging to achieve those bigger, bucket-list adventures - vacation day limits, financial constraints, and a lack of job security can make longer, more ambitious trips feel impossible. Yet these are the type of trips many of our employees dream of and do!

Our MEC Adventures sabbatical program is one way Mountain Equipment Company supports our staffers in living our purpose of connecting with the outdoors. MEC staffers can apply for an extended unpaid leave from work, ranging from a minimum of 3 weeks to a maximum of 6 consecutive months, to complete an epic outdoor adventure. Staffers can also apply for additional funds or gear to support their trip through the application process.

The best part? Their job will be waiting upon their return... as well as a bevy of teammates eager to hear tales of adventure! MEC Staffer Hannah Spackman13, recently returned from an epic 3-month adventure hiking and exploring in South America.

"I am extremely grateful to work at a company that supports and encourages their employees to get outdoors and explore. I got to use a lot of the camping gear we sell here at MEC on my trip and also saw a lot of other Canadian travelers with MEC gear as well. It was awesome to see our amazing products out there in the wild!"

#LiveYourPurpose #OutdoorLife #EpicAdventures #Sabbatical #LifeChangingTrips #MECStaffPerks"

Source: LinkedIn[14]

"Despite everything,
no one can dictate
who you are to
other people."

PRINCE

YOUR TURN: WHAT IS YOUR MESSAGING SAYING ABOUT YOUR BRAND?

In 2022, my marketing agency, Forge & Spark Media, underwent a strategic refresh. We updated our branding, our website design, and our content strategy to focus on reaching purpose-led businesses like B Corps and social ventures and to emphasize what we're best at, which is crafting strategy and content that builds trust and authority in a given space.

We loved the way we looked and sounded. But for about six months after launching our website, I realized that we were getting some strange leads coming in—organizations who weren't at all aligned with our values and/or who didn't fit our ideal client criteria. They were also asking us a lot of questions about digital marketing and advertising, services that are not our core offering. Something was off. What were we saying—or not saying well—about ourselves to give people the wrong impression?

We explored our site analytics and social media demographics but couldn't pinpoint anything. We looked into our Search Engine Optimization, too, and did find a few misleading keywords in our content, which we replaced with more accurate ones. We also found a few ways to insert much stronger and more accurate keywords into our SEO metadata. But this was by no means the whole story.

Still puzzled, I thought I'd reach out to ChatGPT, asking the AI 'guru' what it understood our brand to be saying and communicating across our channels. In other words, I asked it to analyze what our brand messaging was and how we were coming across in our content.

Initially, the prompt I entered was this:

> Looking at forgeandspark.com and the instagram page instagram.com/forgeandspark, what are the brand's key messages?

This is what I got back:

- **Content Marketing Expertise:** Conveys that it understands the complexities of content marketing strategies and tactics, and it can help businesses navigate the tricky content marketing landscape to achieve their marketing goals. This message is communicated through content focused on topics like SEO, content marketing, social media marketing, social media advertising, and data-driven marketing.

- **Creative and Innovative Solutions:** Highlights its ability to think outside the box and develop unique strategies and campaigns that set its clients apart from the competition. The emphasis may be on creativity, storytelling, and utilizing cutting-edge content marketing techniques to engage audiences effectively.

- **Results-Driven Approach:** Emphasizes its commitment to delivering measurable outcomes and helping clients achieve their business objectives. This message might be reinforced through testimonials, case studies, or metrics showcasing successful campaigns and the impact they have had on the clients' businesses.

Intriguingly—and worryingly—none of the messaging that I *thought* we were putting out there about purposeful messaging, authenticity in marketing, or who we serve was actually being picked up. So, I set out to address that in a series of blog posts, by adjusting my website copy, and by including a specific story pillar in our 2023 marketing plan around purpose and authenticity.

Following this experiment, I got more specific in my prompt to see what we were 'putting out there' on our website specifically. Here's the prompt:

What are five key messages that are being communicated about Forge & Spark Media on the website www.forgeandspark.com?

And here's a summary of what I got back:

- **They are a full-service content marketing agency that helps businesses grow:** Forge & Spark Media positions themselves as a one-stop-shop for all content marketing needs, offering a range of services that help businesses build their brand, attract customers, and increase revenue.

- **They are experts in content strategy and storytelling:** The company emphasizes their expertise in content strategy and storytelling, highlighting their ability to create compelling, engaging content that resonates with audiences and drives results.

- **They have a collaborative and client-focused approach:** Forge & Spark Media emphasizes their collaborative approach to working with clients, highlighting their commitment to understanding their clients' unique needs and goals and working together to achieve them.

- **They have a track record of success:** The company showcases case studies and testimonials that demonstrate their ability to deliver results for clients, positioning themselves as a trusted partner for businesses looking to grow.

- **They are passionate about helping businesses succeed:** Forge & Spark Media communicates a sense of passion and enthusiasm for helping businesses succeed, positioning themselves as a company that genuinely cares about their clients' success and is committed to delivering value.

Better! We moved from talking about results to customer success more broadly (see our messaging), we see the 'trusted partner' language coming up, and we see the language around 'collaboration and client-focused approach.'

Anecdotal evidence is compelling too—your survey of how you're showing up as a brand can and should most certainly extend to real people. The way I do this most frequently is to keep tabs on what people are saying about us online and to ask people directly. We'll learn more about both 'message mining' and gaining audience insights in Chapter 6.

Next up, we'll explore the messaging framework you'll be introduced to in this book.

CHAPTER 2

THE FORGE & SPARK MESSAGING FRAMEWORK AND HOW TO USE IT

Whether you're launching a new company, product, or service or working on growing or evolving an existing one, a messaging framework helps define what your business does, why it matters, and how you deliver value to your audiences and customers.

So, what exactly is a messaging framework? It's a structured guide that you create for yourself and your teams that encapsulates your brand's identity and the unique value you offer. Your messaging framework will be utterly unique to you, assisting you with consistent communication, truly understanding your business, and clearly articulating its purpose to your audience.

A well-crafted messaging framework can become a foundation for your communications work—everything from your content strategy and marketing campaigns to your sales and promotional materials. It can empower you to ensure customers understand who you are and what makes you different. It can equip your sales team with the tools to highlight those differentiators and give your marketing team a solid base to build all future content. And aligning your marketing and sales teams with a clear, consistent messaging framework can significantly improve your ability to close deals and do so more efficiently.

Compelling, right? Let's look first at what makes a good messaging framework, and then at how you'll develop your messaging throughout this book.

The Core Elements of Good Messaging

For a lot of marketers, there's a big gap between what they know (specifically about their brand, goals and customers) and the content they create. They can have intimate knowledge about their business, and still not know what to create in today's LinkedIn post. And this gap is often caused bu missing or unclear messaging. Good messaging, in short, helps you clarify exactly what you need to say to get to where you as a business need to go.

Good messaging is rooted in your purpose, values, mission, and products and services, and is and is based on the business and Content Objectives you identify and the key audiences you most want to reach, engage, and sell to. Good messaging will communicate who you are and what you offer to the audiences that need your offerings—ideally, in a way that resonates with them and makes them feel understood and known by you and your team.

I believe that good, authentic brand and product messaging includes the following core elements.

It Expresses What Guides You

Here's the purpose question: what leads you, every day, to do what you do as a leader, brand, or business? Great messaging is founded on answering this, both subtly and overtly.

Good Messaging Reflects Your Values

There are places you need to get to. Your values guide your decisions and actions along the way—and are well worth expressing in your content and communications.

It's Action-Based

Really good messaging is rooted in 'walking the walk.' Saying something is one thing, and taking action is another. Ideally these are aligned. If not, consider how you can do more of what you say and how you might express more of what you do.

It Offers Proof

It's not enough to talk yourself up. People need to understand who you are as a brand, see proof of what you say, and know you've taken action. Tell stories. Show off your photos and videos—and do an expressive dance if you've got one. If you're a B Corp, this includes pointing out what you've done, for example, to align with Environmental, Social, and Governance (ESG) factors, which are central to B Corp Certification. You get the picture.

It Inspires or Prompts Action

In content marketing, prompting action from your audience is key. Messaging is a crucial part of this. A good messaging framework should be clear about your desired outcomes. Your messaging should include stories that prompt action to encourage your audience to work towards your purpose.

Good Messaging Cares for Your Audience

Really good messaging focuses on your audience's needs and desires. It involves empathy: understanding their challenges and frustrations (what we will call "pain points"), and what they value and need most. An empathetic approach in your communication and marketing will help ensure your messages resonate personally. This matters.

It Connects Emotionally

When you care for your audience, you create an opportunity for connection. Effective messaging and resulting storytelling can make the most of this opportunity, leveraging what you know they want and need to deliver all the feels. Messaging that taps into your audience's emotions can be particularly powerful in building community and fostering long-term relationships.

It's Specific to You

If your messaging could come from anybody other than you, it's not good. Always avoid the broad and the vague, choosing instead to craft impact-focused and specific messages about your brand, products, services, and values in a way that's utterly unique to you.

It's Adaptable

Good messaging must be adaptable to different contexts and channels for it to work. I'll show you how to craft variations of your core messages to suit various formats, such as social media, email, website content, and advertisements. Testing different versions and iterating based on feedback will help refine your messaging for maximum impact.

It's Actionable and Useful

Once you've ensured that your messaging is clear, compelling, and understood by those who will use it, you can then take care to ensure it actually gets used. You can, for example, create clear messaging guidelines for your teams. Or add your important messaging to a centrally accessible team document, like your Employee Handbook, so that everyone understands what you're all about, and uses the same language to convey that in their own communications.

After all, in addition to applying your messaging for outbound marketing, your messaging framework can and should serve as a tool for communicating internally so that your sales and marketing teams, as well as everyone else, are aligned in understanding, believing in, and living your brand's spirit and values.

It's Clear and Consistent

Good messaging will help you maintain consistency across different platforms and audiences. It will also allow you to address your audience in other contexts to avoid confusion and build a recognizable brand identity.

It's Authentic

Good message feels right, true, and unique to you. Authentic messaging is rooted in your brand's purpose and values and fundamentally in who you are as a brand or person. It should reflect who you are as a brand, avoiding any possible manipulation or duplicity. Authenticity not only builds trust but also fosters genuine connections with your audience.

Developing Your Messaging Framework

Our process for creating effective purpose-driven brand messaging, developed and refined over the past decade, involves the following stages, which we'll move through in the following chapters of this book.

Purpose & Values: Getting clear on your 'why' will serve as the foundation of your messaging and content marketing.

Content Marketing Mission & Goals: Defining your content marketing mission and setting clear Objectives and Key Results (OKRs) for your content marketing will bring clarity about what you most need your messaging and marketing to do for your business and brand.

Audience Insights & Personas: With the help of audience insight gained through research and interviews, you'll next define your target audiences, one at a time, and understand their jobs, pain points, and desired gains regarding your content. Your audience is not just a recipient of your messaging and marketing, but a contributor to your business success, so understanding their needs and preferences is critical.

Core Brand Messaging and Messaging 'Recipes': What You Have to Say-Uniquely: Stemming directly from your goals and audience personas, you'll next determine the value proposition of your content and create messaging statements and recipes that are actionable and effective. This stage includes developing your Core Brand Message and other key messages necessary for your business.

Developing Your Content: In this stage, you'll use the messaging you've developed to determine what you'll create content about, and how you'll express you brand. It will include identifying your Story Pillars, Messaging Themes, and Content Formats, so that you can craft on-brand (and on-purpose) content to reach your audience, and your own goals.

CONTENT
Story Pillars, Themes, & Content Formats

MESSAGING
Brand Messages & Messaging 'Recipes'

AUDIENCE
Audience Insights & Personas

GOALS
Mission & OKRs

**MESSAGING
FOUNDATION**
Your Brand's Purpose & Values

How Our Messaging Framework Works

I've created the messaging framework in this book as a guide to help you articulate your brand's heart and soul—all in a practical and actionable way (I am a Capricorn, after all).

It's designed to give equal weight to what truly makes your brand, products, or services unique **and** what your audience needs and wants from you. These two things are balanced in this framework so that you can communicate and create content in a way that resonates with and benefits your audience, and grow your business and brand while you're doing it.

At the heart of your messaging, I hope, will be clarity, authenticity, and purpose—principles that guide you in creating messaging that doesn't just sell what you do, but that genuinely connects with the people you care about doing business with, too.

We start by getting to the core of your brand's purpose—your 'why.' This isn't just a box to check; it's the foundation of everything you do. Understanding your 'why' gives your messaging direction and meaning, helping you craft stories that matter. This clarity becomes your north star, aligning your content marketing efforts with your brand's mission and values and ensuring every word you share feels true to who you are.

You'll begin by getting to the core of your brand's purpose—your 'why.' In content and communication, purpose is the foundation of everything you do and say. And understanding and being able to articulate your 'why' in various ways will give your messaging direction, humanity, and meaning, helping you craft stories that matter to real people while ensuring every word you share feels true to who you are.

From there, I'll ask you to get clear on what you want to achieve with your messaging and marketing. You'll define your content marketing mission statement, and set clear Content Objectives and Key Results. You'll then work on identifying and empathizing with your most important audiences: the people you most wish to communicate with, so that you have a clear understanding about what they're trying to accomplish, their challenges, and how your brand or business can help.

By seeing the world through their eyes, you'll get clarity on what they most need to hear from you so that you can craft valuable and resonant messages that offer solutions and a sense of being seen and understood. This is where the juicy stuff happens—crafting a unique value proposition and foundational brand messages that highlight what makes your brand stand among your competitors while remaining genuine.

With your core messaging in place, the framework then guides you in crafting the kinds of messages you and your team will use everyday and everywhere. You'll create messages that can be used anywhere you need them—whether it's your own LinkedIn profile, your business website or social media, or marketing collateral. I'll show you how to create your own Messaging Recipes that apply your core messaging precisely where you need it to create customized messages for various occasions and needs.

Finally I'll guide on how to express all this messaging in your ongoing content marketing, using it to define your Story Pillars, Themes, and Content Formats.

The book concludes there, but your messaging won't. I always recommend ongoing testing, refining, and tweaking. Your messaging isn't a one-and-done deal; it evolves with your brand and the world around you. By continuously listening, adjusting, and learning, you'll keep your communication fresh, relevant, and effective, ensuring your audience feels connected and engaged.

CHAPTER 3

THE PURPOSE OF PURPOSE ...
AND HOW TO DEFINE YOURS

"I've given it a lot of thought, and I've decided what I'm really missing at this point in my life is to form a meaningful relationship with a purpose-driven paper towel brand. I'm telling you, finding a paper towel brand that stands for something and then following, liking, re-posting, and creating user-generated content for it is the best decision I've made in a long time. The only question I have now is: What purpose should this paper towel brand have?"

—John Long, *McSweeney's Magazine*

Right. So, maybe don't invent a purpose for your brand just to jump on the next hot marketing trend.

That said, if you—as a business or marketing leader—are genuinely driven to make your corner of the world a little more sustainable, equitable, friendly, helpful, or kind, I offer a sincere thank you for that because what you're doing matters.

How you're talking about it matters, too.

As an individual, I'm sure you've been challenged by someone you know to improve the world somehow, with helpful or positive results. I certainly have been inspired, changed, prodded to action, and otherwise kicked in the butt by individuals in my life. So, I know that what we do and say as individuals can affect and change those around us. We know that real change in the world can be effected by one person, one idea, one intention. Until recently, it just hadn't occurred to me that the same applied to businesses.

In my younger years, I thought founding, managing, and growing a business was a Big, Important, Complex thing. Business is cold, I used to think. It's impersonal. It's opaque. It's boring. It's about money, cogs, and workin' 9 to 5 (sing it, Dolly).

But my business isn't any of those things. And since you're reading this book, I'm guessing that yours probably isn't either.

And sure, those things can be a part of running a business. There's plenty of slog. And effort. And hard work. But in running one's own business, there is a choice. Thank Jebus.

I run a content agency. As I think of it, the long and short of it is that I help people—specifically people building businesses to create positive social impact—figure out what to say and how to say it authentically to grow their business. I do this very intentionally for a couple of reasons. First, I'm good at it. Second, people who are trying to effect positive change don't always know how to talk about it and need my help. And third, I believe my work is important beyond just selling stuff or fulfilling a service.

That third bit—that I believe that what I do is important in some way— is the "house" for my purpose. Maybe yours, too. And I've always had to dig a bit to figure out why.

My digging looks a little like this.

On a human level, I know how much authentic expression matters and what the price is for a person who feels like they can't show up as they truly are or doesn't feel seen, known, or accepted in the world. I know how much it matters to say what's true. To tell others what you honestly think and believe. To show others who you are and what's important to you.

And yes, I believe this also applies to our brands' communication and marketing.

As marketers, we should always aim to reach and engage real people. Even when we're executing on the 144th step of an automated campaign, we'd do well to consider that **one person at a time is paying attention to what we're saying.**

And good gravy, why would we—the person trying to talk to that person, communicate, and drive a particular result—want to come off as a manipulative, pompous, or aggressive complete jerk? I don't. And I'm guessing you don't, either. And yet, I get those emails. I read those social posts. I skim those blogs. And a little piece of me feels insulted, saddened, or patronized almost every time.

We can be better than that. We can be ourselves.

For me, this purpose—simply doing what I can to bring authenticity and genuine connection to communication on both a personal and a professional level—drives me. It makes my business not feel like a business. It makes me feel good about what I do.

It also resonates with the people who hire me. And that's good for business.

Purpose is the foundation.

> *"Don't shrink. Don't puff up. Stand your sacred ground.*
>
> —Brené Brown, *The Gifts of Imperfection*

Yep, I'm one of those people who loves Brené Brown. She's outspoken, honest, vulnerable, and smart. She sounds like nobody else I've ever come across. She sounds like herself. And she's got a clear purpose.

You might think that Brown's purpose is helping people communicate more clearly. Or to express their vulnerability. Or to be able to speak up about shame. Nope. She says, "I'm not here to make people comfortable or to be liked. My purpose is to know and experience love. This means excavating the unsaid. In the world and in me."

Our purpose should guide us as individuals, professionals, organizations, and brands.

If you've lost or have never found yours—as a business leader, a business or brand owner, or a leader in charge of communicating or marketing a business or brand—you're in the right place. In subsequent chapters, we'll explore how to pin down your purpose and use it to ground you in how you communicate.

Because communicating with authenticity—communication that is rooted in your purpose and values—to connect genuinely with other people is, as The Mandalorian says, "The way," I'll do my best to guide you there.

Unpacking Purpose

Purpose is a form of meaningful intention. It helps us define, achieve, and focus on what matters to us in life and in our careers or businesses.

Because it crystallizes what matters most to us, purpose also helps us set and organize our priorities. It can help us define what we want and need in our lives (work and otherwise) and can also aid us in sorting out what to say no to and in making decisions.

When I think of someone with purpose, I think of someone with energy, drive, and vision—someone who knows what they want and who maintains focus on that thing or things, even in the face of adversity. A purposeful person is not someone who skips from thing to thing without reason or thought or who gets easily distracted because their purpose guides and drives them forward.

In business, a clear purpose offers clarity and direction to various stakeholders, ensuring that everyone involved is not only working towards the same business goals but also has a shared intention and understanding of why they—and everyone else—should care about those goals.

A Few Kinds of Purpose-Driven Organizations (and Leaders)

A purpose-driven organization is a business that goes beyond just making money. It's about positively impacting society and the environment while running a successful operation.

And you know what? A purpose-driven *leader* can be found everywhere, not just within purpose-driven organizations. Anyone who leads a team, big or small, with a meaningful purpose that goes beyond just making a profit. Purpose-led leaders and organizations use their influence to inspire others and make a difference.

Here are a few examples of organizations that fit this description.

B Corps

A B Corp is like a for-profit business with the conscience of a non-profit. These companies, which must be certified by B Lab, are focused on making a positive impact on society, the environment, and the people they connect with. As such, they are required to meet social and environmental standards and are legally bound to think about how their decisions affect their workers, customers, suppliers, community, and environment. Examples of well-known global B Corps include Ben & Jerry's, Patagonia, and Coursera. Lesser-known but equally inspiring B Corps include Poppy Barley, Cheekbone Beauty, Birch Bark Coffee Company, Sisters Sage, and The Unscented Company. These companies are dedicated to sustainable practices, supporting Indigenous communities, promoting inclusivity, and balancing profit with purpose in their business models.

Social Ventures

Social ventures are businesses that tackle social or environmental challenges while making a profit. From a purpose perspective, a typical social venture should address a social or environmental problem while also generating profit and staying in business. Like B Corps, these ventures set out to make a positive impact along with succeeding financially, and they tend to operate in sectors like healthcare, education, renewable energy, and sustainable agriculture. Social ventures can be either for-profit or non-profit/not-for-profit and may use various business models, including social enterprises, cooperatives, and benefit corporations. Social ventures do not have the specific legal structure B Corps do that requires them to meet specific social and environmental standards. Examples of social ventures include Grameen Bank (providing microloans to impoverished individuals in Bangladesh to promote entrepreneurship and alleviate poverty), The Big Issue (a UK-based magazine offering homeless and vulnerably housed people the opportunity to earn an income through selling the publication), and **Lucky Iron Fish (**a Canadian company providing iron fish that can be added to cooking pots to combat iron deficiency and improve global health affordably and sustainably).

Not-for-Profits

Not-for-profit organizations (NPOs) are entities organized for a purpose other than generating profits for owners or shareholders. Typically, NPOs are focused on a social or charitable mission, and any profits generated are reinvested in the organization to further its mission. They might be structured as charities, foundations, or associations, and they rely on donations, grants, and other forms of funding to support their operations. Distinct from B Corps or social ventures, NPOs are **not** focused on generating profits for their owners or shareholders but rather on achieving their social or charitable mission.

A few examples of not-for-profits include Benetech, which develops technology solutions addressing social issues such as literacy, human rights, and environmental conservation; Pathways to Education, which offers academic, financial, and social support to youth in need, significantly improving graduation rates in various communities across Canada; and the Canadian Legacy Project, which supports Canadian veterans living in poverty by providing housing, support services, and community integration initiatives.

Charities

Charities tend to tie their organizational purpose directly to their activities; their purpose is to provide direct assistance to individuals or communities in need. They're generally organized around a specific cause or issue, such as poverty, education, or healthcare, and tend to rely on donations, grants, and other forms of funding to support their operations and programs.

Examples of inspirational charities I love include Dress For Success, empowering women to achieve economic independence by providing a network of support, professional attire, and development tools; Room to Read, which focuses on improving literacy and gender equality in education in low-income countries; and Children's Aid Foundation of Canada, which supports vulnerable children and youth in the child welfare system by providing resources and opportunities to help them thrive.

Self-Defined Purpose-Driven Brands and Leaders

Yep, you guessed it: Anybody with a clear purpose can be a purpose-led brand or leader and shout from the rooftops about it. In general, though, you may not want to do much shouting (or marketing) if your purpose isn't particularly admirable or clear. So, if you want to assume this mantle yourself, just ensure that your purpose is clear, meaningful, and resonates with people you care about doing business with.

The Three Senses of Purpose in Business

Purpose is valuable, but it can be tough to define, as is highlighted in the excellent HBR article "What Is the Purpose of Your Purpose?" by Jonathan Knowles, B. Tom Hunsaker, Hannah Grove, and Alison James.

The authors look at the 'three purposes of a purpose used by businesses and brands today." For them, it breaks down to Competence, Cause, and Culture.

"Purpose has become something of a fad and a victim of its own success. Companies are aware that their customers and employees are paying more attention to it as part of a wider reassessment of the role of corporations in society. BlackRock's CEO, Larry Fink, and other major investors are urging executives to articulate a role for their companies beyond profit making, implying that doing so will affect their valuation. But despite its sudden elevation in corporate life, purpose remains a confusing subject of sharply polarized debate. Our research indicates that a primary cause of this confusion is that "purpose" is used in three senses: competence ("the function that our product serves"); culture ("the intent with which we run our business"); and cause ("the social good to which we aspire")."

The authors note that cause-based purposes typically receive the lion's share of attention "largely because companies that push for societal change are more visible," However, each of the three types can be seen in the business landscape today.

Zappos, for example, was a prominent poster brand for culture-based purposes. Their purpose statement, "To Live and Deliver WOW" places the company's heart and soul in service and going above and beyond for customers. Indeed, the company's early marketing and storytelling told that story brilliantly.

In 2011, for example, a customer called Zappos after ordering six pairs of shoes for her mother, whose feet were sore from medical treatments. She was looking to return the shoes, but instead of simply processing a return, Zappos went well above and beyond.[15] They sent the customer's mother a bouquet of flowers with a get-well-soon message and, soon after, upgraded her, her daughter, and her sister to VIP accounts, giving them all free expedited shipping for future orders. This gesture speaks volumes about Zappos' values in action: the team went well beyond customer service to express genuine empathy while taking meaningful action to establish what must have been an emotional connection in alignment with their brand purpose of delivering "WOW" experiences.

Cause-based purpose? Look no further than Patagonia. As we've already discussed, their well-known purpose statement, "in business to save our home planet," highlights that their main purpose is their cause.

Lastly, HBR cites Mercedes as exemplifying competence-based purpose. With its purpose to "First Move the World," the authors note that the brand "expresses a clear value proposition to customers and the employees responsible for delivering on it."

The bottom line? Purpose-driven businesses have clarity around their 'why,' which guides their actions and decisions and arguably strengthens their brand and messaging. Clarity is key. It's like having a business sense of self.

And this clarity of purpose pays dividends, enabling businesses like yours to:

- Attract and retain like-minded employees, contractors, or free-lancers who are equally passionate about your purpose and mission

- Attract, engage, and perhaps build stronger connections with customers who share similar values

- Stay focused on the real goal, avoiding 'shiny object syndrome,' and driving real innovation that aligns with your core purpose

- Navigate decision-making, business challenges, and industry changes/conditions using a clear, consistent moral compass

- Create a work environment that feels genuinely good

- Differentiate your brand from competitors

- Do some good: contribute in what you feel is a positive way to your society, community, and/or the environment, with a strong reputation and brand approval

Clarify and focus on your real, genuine 'why,' and get set to navigate your business journey, all while staying true to your core values and mission.

How Purpose Can Benefit Business—And How False Purpose Can Harm

Doing good can make for good business. Consumers will spend their money with value-aligned companies. And because business owners want to attract those consumers, they might be tempted from time to time to play up their brand's do-goodery in a way that's not entirely true. 'Purpose-washing' describes companies that claim to be purpose-driven or socially responsible but are not committed to creating positive social or environmental impact.

Greenwashing is the first and best-known example of this. Brands that greenwash claim to be sustainable and/or environmentally friendly without truly walking the walk. Their products or operations might do more harm than good, or their claims (e.g., that their products are made with recycled materials) may prove decidedly false (e.g., only a small percentage of the materials are recycled).

Poor cause marketing or tokenism may represent another group of examples around purpose-washing, and it's one to be mindful of when creating purpose-led messaging and marketing. Questionable cause marketing involves using social or environmental causes in various ways to promote your products or services without significantly contributing to the cause. You might, for example, claim to donate to a specific charity or cause—amazing! But if it's not making an impact or only a tiny fraction of your revenue is being donated, you may be crowing about your goodness without really deserving to.

Tokenism, similarly, involves making claims about something that sounds positive (usually environmentally or socially) without truly delivering. McDonald's is a good example, having, in 2018, loudly announced a global goal to source all of its packaging from renewable, recycled, or certified sources by 2025—while critics of the company argue that while the company has made some efforts to reduce plastic waste, such as by eliminating plastic straws in some markets, it continues to use vast amounts of single-use plastic packaging in its restaurants. This is a tricky one, indeed. Talking about the positive social or environmental steps or progress you're making in your marketing can be useful, but if your claims are more talk than action, your marketing efforts may backfire and be perceived as purpose-washing.

As the HBR authors remind us, "Many of the challenges that companies encounter with purpose stem from a perceived lack of alignment between how they behave and what they say they stand for. It is tempting to claim to be "purpose-driven" because of the appeal to employees and consumers—but that works only if you demonstrate authenticity and coherence."

In other words, you've simply gotta walk the walk. Don't claim purpose without having one.

Doing good business requires us to not only attract, serve, and satisfy our customers but also to attract and nurture people within our organizations and to 'do good business,' which, as HBR defines it, is to "conduct business in a manner that secures its license to operate in the eyes of the community and regulators—all while earning an appealing return on capital." At first glance, coming up with a great purpose statement and telling everyone about it can seem like an easy way to convince everyone you've covered all your business bases. But if it's not true from the inside out, you're jeopardizing your branding, marketing, and perhaps your business.

"What you are is what you have been. What you'll be is what you do now."

— BUDDHA

How to Develop a Purpose Statement

If you've already done some thinking about your brand purpose and the impacts you'd like to create in the world or—better yet—have created a Vision or Mission Statement for your brand or business, or have completed any work relating to the Theory of Change, you're ahead of the game as we set out first to create a Purpose Statement for your brand.

Your Purpose Statement should capture the passion behind what you do and why you do it. It's all about your intentions and aspirations, often reflecting core values and beliefs. Because of these qualities, this statement can be of foundational importance for your positioning, messaging, and storytelling.

Developing clarity about what drives you should feel both grounding and inspiring. Recall Theodore Roosevelt's excellent advice: "Keep your eyes on the stars, but your feet on the ground."

Let your purpose serve as your foundation: the force that both grounds, and motivates you to become, and express, what you're most meant to be.

To define or clarify your own purpose statement (personal or otherwise), consider trying one of the short exercises below.

Approach One: Keep On Asking Why

Pretty much anyone who's ever encountered a child knows how hard it is to answer why. *Why is the sky blue? Why do planes stay in the air? Why do I have to go to bed?*

But you know what? Answering your series of 'why' questions might be even more challenging.

Why are you in the business you're in? Why are you convinced—or not—that what you do matters? Why do you keep at it every day, or why do you feel discouraged? When was the last time you felt passionate, excited, and optimistic ... and why did you feel that way?

Why questions can reveal important answers about your purpose, especially if you dig deep. Purpose is what you care about deeply and want to contribute to the world. The big problem or challenge you'd like to devote your time, attention, and unique set of skills to helping solve. It's what, at the end of every month, day, or year, if we didn't do it, we wish we'd done.

Goals, objectives, and intentions are related but are smaller steps that serve your purpose.

If you're a big goal-setting fan, you can use something like the 'five whys' approach[16] to interrogate those goals and intentions to get close to your root cause or your purpose. Here's an example I wrote about for our blog a few years ago, updated for this book.

Inspired by reading books like Charlotte's Web in Grade 1, writing a book is on my list of life goals.

Why?

The ability to help or inspire others is inspiring to me. And to create new worlds in words seems like magic to me. I want to be a part of that.

Why?

I've seen the power and impact of storytelling. It changes minds. It can change lives.

Why? How?

Reading or listening to others' worlds and thoughts can inspire me, and make me feel like there are others out there who think like me, who want what I want, who have ideas about how to do the things I strive for.

Why?

They have the courage to clarify their thinking, or share their feelings, putting it out for others to experience and learn from. It's bloody brave, and it matters.

Why does it matter?

It's like being the first to raise your hand, or head out to the dance floor. It might just be you, but maybe others will be inspired, join in, express their unique 'take' on the world, too. There's an opportunity for joy, understanding, and connection.

Conversely, having lost people in my life to depression and suicide, I know the devastation of staying silent, and the price one can pay for a false sense of acceptance or belonging.

That's it. The price of not expressing oneself is far too high, compared with the opportunity for joy and connection that authentic expression can offer.

The incredible thing is that I've done this exercise at different times, starting from different goals, and my answers—usually about five 'whys' in—are always eerily similar.

My personal 'why,' which extends to my leadership and work, revolves around using the magical powers of communication, storytelling, and honest, authentic expression to connect people and promote belonging. That's just something I feel deeply and know, in my core, is important in my life.

So perhaps it's not overly surprising that the business I created has a purpose statement that's very similar to my own. It's not the same, but its roots are commingled.

At Forge & Spark, our purpose is to foster genuine connection, even in marketing.

To this brief statement I often provide an expanded statement high-lighting the impact this purpose creates:

We bring authenticity and impact to brand messaging and marketing content so that companies with purpose can grow, thrive, and change the world

Our purpose statement is designed to be short and sweet so that everyone in our company—as well as our audiences—can remember it, 'get it', and share it comfortably and confidently.

It's cheeky, acknowledging that a lot of marketing content kind of sucks, while also showing that we get that, and that we're trying to do better. The statement is also meant to capture the importance we (and I) place on human connection, and how that drives what we do. Connecting people in a genuine way is our why.

What's yours?

As you consider your purpose in the context of your marketing, it's helpful to review and reflect on any existing documentation you may already have around mission, vision, and values. If these statements are already fine-tuned, and helpful to you in expressing your brand purpose, you are in great shape for completing your messaging.

Your organization may also have completed work relating to the Theory of Change, a methodology used by organizations and teams to plan and evaluate initiatives for creating social impact. If so, you could use this strategic planning tool, which maps out the logical sequence of programs initiatives to show how and why a desired change is expected to happen, as a starting point for your content marketing and storytelling. You might, for example, look at using your Theory of Change work to help define purpose, core brand messaging, and the definition of Story Pillars and themes for your content marketing.

I will say that I do this exercise—and the one following—every couple of years just to be sure I'm clear and on the purposeful path I want to be on.

Particularly after a business has grown and evolved, refreshing your purpose statement can be a clarifying exercise. We all get lost in the busyness of days and the minutiae of running businesses, balancing families, and being amazing. We have to be profitable. We have to pay our employees. Sometimes, we like to pay ourselves. So, sometimes, purpose gets a bit muddy in the mix.

Here's my two cents: Profit is essential when running a business. But it's a poor 'why.' It'll motivate you and others for a while, but it sure doesn't make for compelling storytelling.

Approach Two: The Within Way

One of our former clients, Within People, is a consultancy dedicated to helping companies create stronger organizational cultures. They developed a simple and effective framework for developing your purpose statement in a way that I've seen work well for individual leaders as well as small and large businesses. I like it. It's simple. And you'll get good results.

It works by asking yourself—or your team—three key questions:

1. What is the problem in the world you are most passionate about solving?

2. What impact do you make in people's lives by solving that problem?

3. What is your role in making that impact, and how do you solve the problem?

I tested this out recently to refresh our purpose statement at Forge & Spark. I'll share my embarrassingly rough thinking below.

What is the problem in the world you are most passionate about solving?

It's not always easy for leaders or organizations to create effective marketing that feels aligned with their values. Sometimes, this comes down to not knowing what to say or how to say it. Sometimes, there's fear about sounding overly 'salesy' or preachy. And sometimes, it's a matter of not having the skill, time, or people to carry off consistently effective marketing.

What impact do you make in people's lives by solving that problem?

Ultimately, effective, on-brand marketing enables these excellent, purpose-inspired businesses to grow and flourish, while staying true to their values.

This one was interesting for us to workshop because we have long discussed the results we achieved in our marketing and messaging. And that's a necessity—it IS why people seek us out. But I think it's critical to our uniqueness that we care as much about authenticity and generating real authority and trust as about marketing results. Getting clarity here has changed our messaging and content and how I think about the business.

What is your role in making that impact, and how do you solve the problem?

With our clients, we serve as trusted advisors and there-for-you partners, giving them the tools, training, and/or hands-on support they need to show up with integrity in their marketing and get results. Really good content marketing isn't easy to do alone, so we partner with them every step of the way—from strategy right through to the granular details of posting and captioning—to ensure they develop authentic marketing they're proud of.

Our resulting statement?

"We empower purpose-driven businesses to grow and thrive with authentic, values-aligned marketing that builds trust, fosters pride, and creates meaningful connections with the right customers and communities."

It's a work in progress, as yours might be, too. I encourage you to test it out using the structure outlined below.

Grounding purpose	
Your purpose statement captures the passion and purpose behind what you do as a business -- and should contribute to your positioning, messaging, and storytelling.	
What problem in the world are you most passionate about solving?	
What impact do you make in people's lives by solving that problem?	
What is YOUR role in making that impact, and how do you solve the problem?	

Grounding purpose	
Consider drafting a paragraph or so explaining your purpose as a leader or as a brand.	
Can you get it down to a sentence?	
Can you get it down to a phrase—max 10 words?	
YOUR SHORT-FORM PURPOSE STATEMENT	Why you do what you do, simply put: 10 Words or less
DETAILED PURPOSE STATEMENT	A paragraph you'll use on your website, in communications documentation, or in award/ funding/grant applications. Describe your role in helping your customers solve critical problems and make a change in the world beyond the financial.

You can also find a Purpose Worksheet within the full Messaging Map Template at: **https://forgeandspark.com/content-with-purpose**

CHAPTER 4

GET CLEAR ON YOUR CONTENT MARKETING MISSION

So many people I've worked with over the years—from CEOs to solo-preneurs to in-the-trenches marketers—have come to me with the same problem. It goes something like this:

Even though I know my brand, I find myself falling behind in my marketing! When it's time to write a post, I don't know where to begin or what to say. So I end up publishing random content just to keep up. And then of course it doesn't achieve the impact I'd like. Sadly, we seem to do that again and again.

Have you been there? I have.

And here's what I know: When you're throwing up content when you can, you're generally wasting the time you could use for thoughtful strategy and planning. Without strategic planning, you can rarely tell a clear and consistent story or drive towards a clear goal.

In this chapter, we'll develop a **Content Marketing Mission Statement** for your brand. This will set you up to explore your more specific Content Objectives and key results (OKRs) in the following chapter, providing a clear roadmap and relieving the uncertainty you may be feeling.

Where Content Connects to Your Business: Your Content Mission

As we saw in the previous chapter, why you're in business—your business or brand purpose—shapes your business and informs what you'll want to say about it in your marketing. The same is true for the other critical elements of a brand foundation: your corporate values and your company's mission statement.

There are excellent books and resources to help you define these fundamentals for your business; I don't presume to be an authority on any of those. What I can offer here, however, is a glimpse at how these business fundamentals can inform your messaging and marketing.

Purpose, of course, can guide you in telling passion-fuelled stories and sharing insights and expertise that reflect what you're best at and most care about. Similarly, your business (or corporate) values will do much to guide your business decisions and culture, which can be beautifully reflected in the stories you tell about your business and your content.

And your company mission statement – which has been traditionally a stuffy, dusty, painfully dull affair (think: "our mission is to pursue excellence in every aspect of our business" or "to be a leader in our industry through innovation and service") today tends to serve as a bit of a mélange … bringing together your purpose, vision and values along with a soupcon of your 'how' (your customers, what kinds of products/ services you offer) to succinctly communicate your essence.

Patagonia's mission statement, for just one example, is: "Build the best product, cause no unnecessary harm, use business to inspire and implement solutions to the environmental crisis." This statement reflects Patagonia's 'how' (they produce high-quality products— specifically clothing and gear) and a bit of their 'why' (they set out to impact the environment positively). The statement also suggests that businesses can be a force for good and that they've signed up to do just that.

Trust me, crafting a mission statement that has it all can be challenging, but if you can get close, you'll give your marketing team a huge head start in figuring out the best stories to tell about your brand, providing a clear focus for your content strategy.

When your marketing team or brand content creators understand your purpose and values, they know why you do what you do. This allows them to more passionately and authentically support and talk about your brand and the value or positive impact you have on the world.

After all, as the Purpose 2020: Inspiring Purpose-Led Growth report[17] discovered, "Today, employees want to do more than sell cars. And today, customers want to do more than buy cars."

Understanding the big-picture positive impact your organization seeks to achieve can help craft compelling and meaningful stories through your content.

How to Craft Your Content Marketing Mission

Unlike your company mission statement, I like to remind teams that your content marketing mission statement doesn't have to be formal or fancy. Your content marketing mission statement is a concise declaration of your content's purpose, target audience, and the value it aims to provide. The formula for crafting your content marketing mission statement is pretty dead simple:

Our content should help **[THIS AUDIENCE]** to **[GET THIS BENEFIT/VALUE]**, so we create **[THIS KIND OF CONTENT]**.

As James Brown wisely advises, let's break it down. Below we'll take a closer look at each component of the formula and how you can fill in the blanks to create your own content marketing mission statement.

YOUR AUDIENCE: WHO IS YOUR CONTENT FOR?

It's impossible to create good content if you don't have a clear picture of who it is for. We encourage you to develop quality personas[18] to better understand and create content for your most important audiences. More on that shortly. But as a starting point, consider a simple approach to creating a 'starter funnel' for your content. Identify:

- One large group of people you would like to make aware of you, your brand, your products or services. For instance, think of these folks at the top of your funnel as potential customers, partners, or advocates. They're people who don't know you yet but should.

- One slightly smaller, more focused group of people who are likely to like, talk about, and buy from (or do business with) you.

Identifying these groups starts you down the road of figuring out what you need to say and do with content to ensure people become aware of you. Then, what you need to say and do with content to ensure that *suitable* leads understand what you offer or do that could benefit them.

After all, engaging a larger audience of people who might like, share, and engage with your content is an excellent way to create more of that second audience, empowering you with the knowledge of who your content is reaching.

MESSAGING SPREADSHEET WORK

Give it a try below on the first part of your content marketing mission:

Our content should help [THIS AUDIENCE]

Remember, keep this broad. Here are a few questions to prompt you, but feel free to ignore any that are not relevant to your brand.

- Who do you broadly need to reach? How do you describe them within your company?

- What are their demographic characteristics (age, gender, location, income level, education, occupation, or industry)?

- What are their main challenges, goals, or aspirations (if your content will address them)?

- How does your product or service fit into their lives, and where will your content fit? (Answering this question might enable you to understand the context in which your audience might use your offerings and your content, inspiring you to zero in on more relevant and targeted content demonstrating your value).

WHAT BENEFIT ARE THEY GOING TO RECEIVE FROM YOUR CONTENT?

This is the part that is not about you or your brand. Rather, it's about your audience and *what they most want and need* from the solution you provide.

You want, after all, to attract the right people to your content. You do this by providing content on topics they're interested in, on the channels they're likely to use, in formats that will attract and engage them. What benefits will they receive from coming across, engaging with, and maybe even sharing your content?

We will explore this topic more deeply when we examine your target audience's needs, but if you're developing a content marketing mission statement for the first time, I encourage you to keep it fairly high-level. Below, I've shared a list of some fairly standard content benefits to get your thinking started.

It educates or solves a problem: Your content teaches your audience something they need, answers common questions that your audience has, and offers a solution to their challenges. Educational content might help your audience develop new skills or improve existing ones, adding tangible value to their lives or businesses. *Content of this* *sort can significantly help position your brand as a trusted authority or resource and inspire gratitude and loyalty.*

It's entertaining: Your content is delightful, funny, or captivating, evoking emotions and perhaps creating memorable experiences. *Content like this can be wonderful for generating initial interest and awareness, engaging audiences, and creating lasting connections to your brand.*

It's beautiful or inspiring: People want and need beauty in their lives and love content that inspires or pleases their senses. *Content like this—much like entertaining content—is great for catching attention, engaging, and developing connections with your audience.*

It's informative and/or helpful: Your content might help your audience make a decision or accomplish something they need to. *This helps build trust and enhance your brand's credibility.*

It provides timely information: Your content might offer your audience news or an update they need to know about at the time they most need it and/or otherwise keep them informed about trends, news, and developments in your industry. *Content like this can engender trust and authority.*

It gives your audience a clear understanding of your products/services: Your content might get right to the point, showing and/or demonstrating the function, impact, and/or benefits of your products or services. *This kind of content helps potential customers understand the value of what you provide and can lead to consideration and sales.*

It helps existing customers: Your content can give them ongoing support, tips, and information. This, of course, helps retain these customers and builds trust and loyalty.

It helps audiences understand you: Your content might dive deep into values, showcase your team or company 'behind-the-scenes,' or exhibit transparency and authenticity. *This allows audiences to see the human side of your brand, which can contribute to purchase decisions and build connection and loyalty.*

MESSAGING SPREADSHEET WORK

Give it a try below:

Our content should help [INSERT YOUR AUDIENCE HERE]

to [GET THIS BENEFIT/VALUE],

Use the list above as a starting point, keeping it high-level and specific to what your brand can confidently offer your audience (that they also want and need).

YOUR KINDS OF CONTENT: WHAT ARE YOU GOING TO PROVIDE?

Thinking of the audience you identified above and the benefits or value they're most likely to appreciate from your brand (and that you can confidently provide), let's start considering what kinds of content you might reasonably offer.

Your content 'sweet spot' is the bridge between what you know and want to share, teach or show; and what your audiences most wants and needs from you.

My best recommendation for determining the kind of content to create is to ensure that it's on-brand and represents a clear intersection of what you know and/or want to offer and what your audience wants and needs from you. That is your content sweet spot. When you hit it, you'll be giving something valuable to your audience—drawing them in—while also showing what you're best at.

This is marketing, after all. So you'll want to get your messaging out there—but you'll want to do it with care and concern for your audience. My guidelines for determining the kind of content to create are simple: remember first what you're trying to accomplish with your marketing, and next, who you most need to reach and engage with it.

You do not have to consider just one kind of content, format, or channel. However, I strongly suggest choosing just one broad focus for your content for now.

Kinds of Content to Consider

Are you interested in showcasing who you are and what you stand for as a brand? Consider **brand-building content and storytelling.**

Consider **problem-solving content** if your audience has a specific problem, challenge, or frustration that your content can help to address. What could your brand knowledgeably and effectively offer related to your products or services?

Consider **format-specific content** if there's a particular format you feel your audience would most appreciate. Think, for example, of written content like blog posts, articles, whitepapers, or ebooks; video content like short fun clips or info-packed tutorials or demos; and so on. Just ensure that whatever format you choose is, again, right for your brand and audience and reasonable for you to produce.

Consider **funnel-stage content** if you're looking to fill or fix a particular gap in your marketing funnel. We generally look at marketing stages as awareness, engagement, consideration, conversation, and loyalty/advocacy. If this is the case, explore the content types that work well for each.

You might consider **platform-specific content** when it's clear the target audience loves or engages, especially with a particular platform, or if you know a specific platform will enable you to achieve a particular objective (e.g., landing pages to encourage efficient consideration and conversion).

Consider **data-driven content** like infographics when your audience needs data, stats, and facts to make decisions.

Do you need them to make that decision? Consider **conversion-focused content** like lead magnets, guides, comparison charts, or templates.

When you already have oodles of articles and content and are looking to ramp up your marketing cost-effectively, you'd do well to consider **repurposed content.** This would maximize your existing investment by updating facts and information, refreshing your SEO, and/or adapting your content for different formats and platforms.

Collaborative content, including user-generated content, influencer partnerships, guest posts, and social media takeovers, should be considered when your audience has stories to tell and if you'd like to build community.

As further fuel for thought, I've gathered the following starter words (a blend of content formats and topics) based on the subject of your expertise:

- How-To Info or Tips About ...

- Strategies for ...

- Stories or Case Studies About ...

- Inspiration and Models for ...

- Testimonials / Real Experiences

- Insights on/from ...

- Strategies for ...

- Reports that describe ...

- Ideas for ...

- Guides or Checklists on ...

- Research on ...

- Events / Webinars / In-Depth Training on ...

MESSAGING SPREADSHEET WORK

Ready? Give it a try below or in your spreadsheet.

Our content should help [INSERT YOUR AUDIENCE HERE]

to [INSERT YOUR BENEFIT/VALUE HERE],

we create [THIS KIND OF CONTENT].

Remember, again, keep this BROAD and consider what your content needs to accomplish for you and what your audience wants and needs from you relating to your offerings.

_____

_____

_____

_____

_____

Sample Content Marketing Mission Statements to Get You Rolling

Below, we've collected a variety of Content Mission Statements in various formats.

Here, for the record, is Forge & Spark's Content Marketing Mission Statement:

Our content helps purpose-led leaders and organizations find and use inspiring, practical, and proven guidance on content marketing practices that yield premium-quality content they can take pride in. With this intention, we create educational and training content, always imbued with personal storytelling, that provides real-life examples and insights always rooted in experience.

Here are a few examples of content marketing missions (we've used our insights to create some, based on our experience of their content, as well as from their purpose statements) from a few prominent brands:

1. **Shopify:** Their content provides entrepreneurs with the insights, inspiration, and tools needed to start, run, and grow their businesses. So much of their content is educational and informative, with a focus on guides, teaching/training, and tools and templates.

2. **Lululemon:** This brand says their content "sets out to elevate the world from mediocrity to greatness" for an audience of health and wellness enthusiasts by sharing stories and ideas that inspire people to live an active, mindful lifestyle.

3. **HubSpot:** Their content helps business owners, marketers, and sales leaders grow their businesses through inbound marketing. They create inspiring and educational content.

4. **Roots Canada:** Roots' content aims to share Canada's rich heritage and culture with the world through stories, products, and experiences.

5. **General Electric:** GE's content aims to help audiences engage in conversations and feel connected through stories of innovation, science, and technology. It creates content that demonstrates how GE is building, powering, moving, and helping the world.

6. **RBC (Royal Bank of Canada):** Their content mission is to provide financial advice, insights, and resources to help our customers make informed financial decisions.

7. **Canadian Tire:** Canadian Tire's content mission is to inspire pride and joy in every Canadian home by sharing helpful, practical, and innovative ideas for home improvement.

8. **Air Canada:** Air Canada's content is targeted at helping travellers and aviation enthusiasts gain insights, stay informed, and feel inspired about travel and aviation. Therefore, they create visually stunning, informative content about places and experiences.

9. **Tim Hortons:** Timmy's (as we refer to the brand in Canada) aims to encourage Canadians and coffee lovers to feel a sense of pride, belonging, and connection to the community. To do so, they create emotionally resonant, community-focused content and stories.

10. **Lush Cosmetics:** Lush's content aims to help customers understand its ethical sourcing, handmade products, and commitment to sustainability while inspiring them to make a positive impact on the world. Therefore, it tends to focus on user-rich stories and influencer content, collaborative content with an activist edge, and content with a unique, compelling style to communicate its brand ethics.

Your Content Marketing Mission

Now that we've covered the three parts of the content marketing mission, it's time to put it all together.

Our content should help [INSERT YOUR AUDIENCE HERE]

to [INSERT YOUR BENEFIT/VALUE HERE],

we create [INSERT YOUR KIND OF CONTENT HERE].

The version of your mission statement above might not feel quite right in this limited format. Try writing it out below in your own words.

_____

_____

_____

"I had no idea that being your authentic self could make me as rich as I've become. If I had, I'd have done it a lot earlier."

OPRAH WINFREY

CHAPTER 5

SETTING CONTENT OBJECTIVES & KEY RESULTS (OKRS)

Your 'why' is the foundation for your messaging, but if you're in business, achieving practical results with your content is vital. In this section, we'll get grounded in how content marketing can help express your purpose *and* meet a few of those necessary business goals, too.

Learning how to set better goals, at least for your content marketing, is a great place to begin.

OKRs: A Modern Approach to Purpose-Driven Success

The OKR Framework is a well-known goal-setting approach used by big players like Google, IBM, LinkedIn, Spotify, Twitter, and companies of all sizes. It's a practical framework that helps teams work together toward goals, relying on a common language to describe the outcomes most important to your business.

According to this framework, first developed by Andy Grove at Intel in the 1970s, *objectives* are clear, inspiring goals, while *key results* are specific, measurable outcomes used to track progress toward these objectives. The idea is to clarify what you're working towards—in the form of a desirable outcome—and then establish how you're going to measure progress towards that specific target.

I personally love the focus on outcomes versus output, which has helped me make decisions on which efforts to prioritize. You can ask yourself whether this or that effort will move us closer to our objective. In your answer, you'll discover your priority.

I've also found OKRs effective in fostering a culture of accountability and continuous improvement—because they're easy to track and record progress against.

Even with small teams and solopreneurs, we've discovered that the framework clicks. Building from your content marketing mission—essentially your broad understanding of what you want your content to be and do—your OKRs enable you to get very specific.

First, they identify the ultimate business objectives you want your content to contribute to and then get clear about your specific objectives for content, with an understanding of exactly how your content should help to achieve those business objectives.

Key results then serve as the compass to track your progress and measure success as you progress toward your objectives.

Finally, what I've added to the mix, for content marketing specifically, is *action*. Action is the juice. Action is also all about defining the tangible steps you, or sometimes your audience, will have to take to accomplish those key results, propelling you closer to your desired objective. Action can also sometimes be called *initiative* or *tactics*. It boils down to what you plan to do to achieve those key results and objectives.

In my own experience in content marketing and goal setting, there has often been a disconnect between what we report on most commonly—things like followership, page views, and likes and shares on social posts, for example—and the actual, accurate results we want to see. These, usually are things like:

- Creating and distributing a genuinely good newsletter consistently

- Improving educational content

- Boosting publishing volume by five posts per month

The OKR system addresses that disconnect by defining the right objectives and the most important key results. When you determine what to measure, you do so with clear intention.

Here's how it all works.

Setting Objectives

Think of your objective as a way to connect your work with your purpose. It's the answer to the question: What exactly do we want to do to deliver on our content marketing mission?

The goal is to identify the most pressing challenge that, if addressed with content marketing, will make the greatest impact on your overall business performance.

A good objective should be about changing something or making something better—not maintaining the status quo. It should feel inspiring, challenging your team to work towards something practical and attainable. And, oh yes, it should have a deadline.

I personally like writing objectives using the old 'headlines from the future' approach. Think first about the period you're giving yourself, say six months. Now, imagine how your content marketing changed during that time. What's the headline or quick statement you'd share in Slack or a newsletter you'd most want to see or share with your team after that period?

Your Business Objective

Pinpoint the most critical issue your business needs to overcome or the most important gain you need to make *that can be addressed with content marketing*. This will be the foundation of your Content OKRs, ensuring that your content marketing efforts address the most pressing challenges for your business—so that your content truly matters.

You—or your boss—will likely have a few business objectives already at the top of your mind. Here are a few very common examples:

Building more brand awareness or becoming better recognized on social media is one very common example of something many businesses want to accomplish—and there's evidence that a good content marketing strategy and operation can really help. Creating a strong presence through compelling, search-optimized blog posts and social media, for example, can attract positive attention and make a brand visible to new audiences.

Another example of a good content-aware business objective is **generating and nurturing leads**, ideally leading to increased sales. Now, content marketing can't always promise sales. However, valuable content can work wonders to educate and inform potential customers, building trust and driving them towards a purchase or some kind of conversion, like booking a call to learn more.

Where to Start?

To identify an optimal business objective for your content marketing, you can begin by taking a good look at your current business performance. Are there any areas where you're underperforming or underwhelming? Are there any potential customers you're not engaging with or selling to?

Another place to start might be looking at your competition and at opportunities or trends in your industry. Are competitors finding sales success through a particular tactic or strategy that you see as possible for you? Or are you seeing your customers suddenly spending time on a new channel or platform that your brand isn't active on?

I'd suggest drafting a few possible business objectives that feel right to you, then involving key stakeholders across departments—such as people from sales, other marketers, and perhaps people who work with your customers directly—to gather various perspectives on where the business needs focus.

If sales have taken a dip, for example, your team might agree that a lack of brand awareness, trust, or engagement might be at fault. If you can't keep customers, you might see the need to focus on more retention-focused communication or marketing to keep customers engaged after a transaction or purchase.

In the end, please ensure that the business objective you zero in on is actionable (from a content marketing perspective), specific enough to act on, and a bit of a stretch, too. A vague objective like "earn more sales and revenue" is an OK starting point, for instance, but "boost revenue by 20% in the next six months by improving lead generation through targeted content" is better.

When you set your business objective, you pave a clear path for your team and content marketing efforts to follow, ensuring that the content and marketing you deliver contributes directly to solving your most pressing business problem.

Your Content Objectives

Your Content Objectives should align with your overarching content marketing mission *and* directly target your business objective. Consider what you need to achieve with content marketing to best deliver on your business objective. And aim to define no more than three clear Content Objectives to guide your planning and content creation. They're a wonderful way to connect your business goals with your team's mission-driven content efforts.

Characteristics of a Good Content Objective

1. **It's change-oriented**: Your objectives aim to improve or transform something rather than maintain the status quo.

2. **It inspires you**: The objective should challenge and motivate your team, pushing them towards something practical and attainable.

3. **It's time-bound**: Ensure you set clear deadlines—I recommend updating objectives each quarter / 90 days.

4. **It's exciting and specific**: Make it exciting and actionable, like a headline you'll read at the end of your efforts.

Sample Content Objectives

Need a starting point for defining your own Content Objectives? Below, I've gathered common examples we've helped our clients develop:

- Increase Brand Awareness / Boost Brand Visibility

- Improve Audience Engagement / Interaction

- Generate (Hopefully Good and Qualified) Leads

- Boost Website Traffic / Drive More Visitors

- Improve Conversion Rates / Get Visitors to Take an Action

- Establish Thought Leadership / Get Known for Expertise

- Expand Newsletter Subscriber Base

- Increase Social Media Followers or Overall Audience

- Boost Customer Retention

- Improve Content Engagement Among a Targeted Audience

Your Key Results

For each Objective, try to identify two to five key results you're hoping for.

Key results should focus on the "how" corresponding to your objectives' "why."

In other words, a good key result should describe how you'll know you're progressing towards your objective. Think about the specific results or outcomes you want to achieve (ensuring that the results you're looking for are aligned with your objective), the kind of progress you want to make in a given period, and broadly, who's accountable for getting it done.

Key Results can be quantitative or qualitative and can focus on growth, performance, revenue, or engagement. An excellent key result should offer a bit of challenge (don't make it too easy to hit) and, of course, be measurable.

Characteristics of a Strong Key Result

For each Content Objective, consider how you'll measure progress. Identify at least one, and no more than five, Key Results for every Objective. Each should:

1. **Offer clear metrics**: Suggest ways to measure progress with specific, quantifiable metrics.

2. **Provide starting and target metrics**: Define a starting or 'baseline' point as well as a target metric so that you can easily track progress.

3. **Be achievable**: Always ensure that the result is realistic and achievable within 90 days (or the period you choose)

4. **Offer up a wee bit of challenge:** Include some sense of challenge to push the team but keep it attainable.

Sample Key Results

Let's look at the sample Content Objectives identified above and pair a sample key result with each.

Objective	Key Result
Increase Brand Awareness	Achieve a 20% increase in brand mentions and social media shares over the next 90 days.
Enhance Audience Engagement	Increase average blog post comments by 15% and boost social media post engagement (likes, comments, and shares) by 10% over the next quarter.
Generate Leads	Increase the number of qualified leads by 25% through lead magnet conversions within three months.
Boost Website Traffic	Increase organic search traffic to key landing pages by 30% within 90 days.
Improve Conversion Rates	Achieve a 10% increase in content-driven conversion rates over the next quarter.
Establish Thought Leadership	Publish five original articles and two whitepapers within three months, achieving at least 500 views per piece.
Expand Newsletter Subscriber Base	Grow the newsletter subscriber base by 20% in the next quarter, with a 10% increase in email open rates.
Increase Social Media Followers	Increase followers on key social platforms (e.g., Instagram, LinkedIn) by 15% over the next 90 days.
Enhance Customer Retention	Increase customer retention rate by 10% over the next six months by engaging current clients with a targeted content series.
Improve Content Engagement	Increase the average time spent on blog posts by 25% and the engagement rate on social media by 20% over the next quarter.

Your Actions / Initiatives

It feels good to get all of that down, yes? For me, it's like a wave of relief to gain clarity about what to focus on and what can be blurred in the backdrop as I set out to achieve my priority objectives.

This next bit, though—identifying your actions and initiatives—is where progress happens. After all, you're unlikely to achieve any objective if you don't take any action.

Looking at each of your key results individually, ask yourself: How will you achieve those results to meet each content objective and your overarching business objective? What initiatives do you need to undertake to deliver those results? Consider what you can do, what your team might do, and what your audience might do to make those Key Rresults a reality.

Jot down everything that initially springs to mind, both at a high level and more granular tasks. Once you have identified several actions/ initiatives, you'll need to determine which ones take priority. Which will deliver the most impact? Are there any simple actions or tasks you might accomplish quickly to see results? Consider your criteria for taking action, and then prioritize your actions and initiatives in the sequence they need to be completed. Finally, break them down into more manageable and assignable tasks.

This process can take time. But even if you start by sketching it all out, for now, you're making progress.

Sample Actions/Initiatives

Again, looking at the sample Content Objectives and key results identified previously, let's explore some sample actions or initiatives that might make it all happen:

Increase Brand Awareness

Key Result: Achieve a 20% increase in brand mentions and social media shares over the next 90 days.

Action/ Initiative: Boost brand visibility by increasing social media mentions and shares by [X%] within [a given time period].

Enhance Audience Engagement

Key Result: Increase average blog post comments by 15% and boost social media post engagement (likes, comments, and shares) by 10% over the next quarter.

Action/ Initiative: Improve audience interaction by increasing either the number or percentage of comments on blog posts by [a set number] over [a given time period].

Generate Leads

Key Result: Increase the number of qualified leads by 25% through lead magnet conversions within three months.

Action/ Initiative: Attract new leads by creating and promoting [X] lead magnets (e.g., guides, gated e-books, or checklists), targeting an [X%] increase in lead generation within three months.

Boost Website Traffic

Key Result: Increase organic search traffic to key landing pages by 30% within 90 days.

Action/ Initiative: Drive more visitors to your website by increasing organic search traffic to key landing pages by [X%] within 90 days.

_____

_____

_____

Improve Conversion Rates

Key Result: Achieve a 10% increase in content-driven conversion rates over the next quarter.

Action/ Initiative: Increase content-driven conversions, perhaps by creating or optimizing landing pages, all to achieve an [X%] increase in conversion rates over the next quarter.

_____

_____

_____

Establish Thought Leadership

Key Result: Publish five original articles and two whitepapers within three months, achieving at least 500 views per piece.

Action/ Initiative: Position your brand as an industry leader by publishing [a set number] of original articles, posts, or whitepapers, and/ or setting up [X] brand-appropriate podcasts within three months.

_____

_____

_____

Expand Newsletter Subscriber Base

Key Result: Grow the newsletter subscriber base by 20% in the next quarter, with a 10% increase in email open rates.

Action/ Initiative: Create lead magnets and email nurture sequences to grow your e-newsletter list by [X%] within [a given time period].

_____

_____

_____

Increase Social Media Followers

Key Result: Increase followers on key social platforms (e.g., Instagram, LinkedIn) by 15% over the next 90 days.

Action/ Initiative: Grow your social audience by boosting your post volume by [X%] on key platforms (e.g., Instagram, LinkedIn) over [a given time period].

_____

_____

_____

Enhance Customer Retention

Key Result: Increase customer retention rate by 10% over the next six months by engaging current clients with a targeted content series.

Action/ Initiative: Improve customer/client loyalty by creating a content series specifically helpful to them (e.g., webinars, tutorials) within the next [a given time period].

_____

_____

_____

Improve Content Engagement

Key Result: Increase the average time spent on blog posts by 25% and the engagement rate on social media by 20% over the next quarter.

Action/
Initiative: Study your demographics and produce more engaging and relevant content for your dominant audience to increase the average time spent on blog posts by [X%] and/or the engagement rate on social media by [X%] over the next [a given time period].

Example OKRs From Forge & Spark

Below, I've included an example of our OKRs, sometimes called OKRAs (OKRs + actions/initiatives), for 90 days, based on boosting sales of our Brand Content Kit service, where we help clients create or elevate their visual branding in a deliciously roll-up-your-sleeves-together week of one-on-one work.

These OKRs came into focus once we got super clear on prioritizing that business objective: to sell 20% more Brand Kits a year. We did that because Lara Kroeker, our Creative Director, absolutely loves working this way with clients—and because this work often leads to our clients asking us to do ongoing content work with them. It sparks joy, and it's good for business. That was clear.

Given our content marketing mission, company purpose, and company values, here are our OKRs within a 90-day window.

Our Content Marketing Mission

Help purpose-led leaders and organizations to find and use inspiring, practical, AND proven guidance on content marketing practices that yield premium-quality content they can take pride in. We aim to create educational and training content imbued with personal storytelling that provides real-life examples and insights based on experience.

A guiding note here: When defining our OKRs, we considered this statement, knowing that we needed to make sure that our OKRs align with our focus on "inspiring, practical, and proven" guidance.

A Key Business Objective We're Working Toward

Sell 24 Brand Content Kit services in the next year (roughly two per month).

90-Day Content Objectives, Key Results, and Actions/Initiatives

Content Objective 1: Publish 3 stories (combining long-form and social) about client benefits from Brand Content Kits within 90 days to generate leads.

Key Results:

- Publish one long-form client success story per month, with a clear CTA linking to the Brand Content Kit sales page.

- Publish at least one short-form social media post about client benefits from brand kits every week, achieving 25 interactions (likes, comments, shares) per post.

- Achieve 500 views per long-form story within the first month of publication.

- Generate at least 10 client inquiries per month from content over the 90-day period with the goal of converting 2 inquiries into sales each month.

Actions/Initiatives:

- **Identify and Survey Clients:** Identify happy clients who benefited from the Brand Content Kit service and gather their feedback and testimonials by email or recorded Zoom calls.

- **Write and Edit Stories:** Incorporate these testimonials into long- and short-form content and refresh the Brand Kit sales page.

- **Design Visuals and Infographics:** Create visuals and infographics to accompany each story to post on social channels (visuals provide good social media engagement).

- **Publish & Promote Stories:** Schedule, publish, and promote stories across blog, social media, email newsletters, and targeted ads.

Content Objective 2: Drive 300 visitors to our Brand Content Kit sales page in the next 90 days to support sales.

Key Results:

- Optimize all published Brand Content Kit blog posts, along with other blog posts that reference our design services, with high-impact keywords by the end of the first month.

- Increase organic search traffic to Brand Content Kit pages, targeting 300 visitors over 90 days (100 per month).

- Get 10 qualified leads via organic search to the sales page within 90 days.

- Target 2+ minutes average session duration on the sales page, adjusting to ensure our content is engaging and helpful.

Actions/Initiatives:

- **Conduct Keyword Research**: Prioritize long-tail SEO keywords for Brand Content Kits and design services, identifying and implementing them in all related posts.

- **Add Targeted Posts to Content Calendar**: Include SEO-driven blog posts and landing page updates in our monthly content calendar and planning discussions.

- **Optimize for SEO**: Implement SEO best practices in all blog posts and all web pages linked to the Brand Content Kit.

- **Share Content**: Promote optimized blog posts and Brand Content Kit pages across social media and email newsletters.

Monitor and Analyze Traffic: Use A/B testing on key landing pages to refine CTAs and increase conversion rates.

Content Objective 3: Boost month-over-month engagement with our Brand Content Kit content across social media and web platforms within 90 days.

Key Results:

- Post high-engagement content related to Brand Content Kits on all active social media platforms at least once per week, with a target of 5 meaningful comments per post.

- Increase followers on Instagram by 100 and 50 on LinkedIn by the end of the 90-day period.

- Achieve an average engagement rate of 7% per post related to Brand Content Kits, with specific focus on shares, comments, and saves.

Actions/Initiatives:

- **Add All Sales Content to Social Media Calendar**: Plan and schedule social media posts focused on Brand Content Kit benefits and testimonials, weaving into our existing calendar and planning.

- **Create Engaging Content**: Develop user-generated content, behind-the-scenes visuals, and client success stories to encourage interaction.

- **Engage with Our Audience:** Actively respond to comments, shares, and DMs about the Brand Content Kit within 24 hours, providing guidance on how to buy the Kit.

- **Analyse Social Media Metrics**: Ensure that we add Kit-specific reporting to our existing monthly analysis, reviewing engagement and adjusting strategies based on high-performing content.

And so far ... It's working well.

Since this is a new service for us, we weren't at all sure what to expect and had nothing to compare it to. So we were guessing when we set both our sales and traffic targets (although we based those targets on our current audience, traffic, and metrics).

So ... after initially trying the service with two generous clients willing to be guinea pigs of sorts for the service, we began generating and publishing organic content (no ads) according to the targets shared above.

Our results? In our first 90 days after releasing the service, we fielded 12 direct inquiries, generated four sales, and have seen good engagement on our posts relating to the Kits—although we didn't hit our engagement targets. We also fell far short of our 2+ minute session duration target on our sales page, indicating that something was off ... so we have just now spent some time improving, testing, and optimizing the content on that page.

Overall, we're really happy with the goals that we set and are working this quarter to knock 'em all out of the park in Q2 of the project. It's all about getting clear on what you want to achieve, the tangible results you most want to see, and what you're going to do to make them happen. Then, you get to play with what you uncover and discover.

The Next Key to OKRs: Actually <u>Measuring</u> Your Progress ... and Success

There's no point to setting OKRs if you're not going to actually pay attention to, or use, your OKRs. And it's so darned easy to skip reporting. But once you're clear on your OKRs, I strongly recommend setting up a way of tracking your progress. Like, right now.

As soon as we set OKRs for ourselves or for our clients, we set up a simple reporting document: either a Google Doc or a Google Sheet. We then look back at the OKRs and document them in such a way that we can report against them each month. You may wish to ensure that you're set up to measure not only MOM progress (month over month) but also QOQ (quarter over quarter) and YOY (year over year) progress so that you don't get caught up panicking when you have a poor month, or overly celebratory when you have a killer month.

A Report Template for Your OKRs

Here, for reference, is a super simple reporting template that you can generate with ChatGPT or another AI tool with the prompt I used below (you can probably come up with a way better one yourself):

Prompt: Based on the following set of Content Objectives, Key Results, and related Actions and Initiatives, please set up a reporting template that allows us to measure our baseline metrics, monthly data for each key result, and includes a space for recording the previous month.

We generated this one using all of the OKRAs established for our Brand Content Kit.

Objective 1: Publish 3 stories about client benefits from Brand Kits within 90 days to generate leads.

Key Result	Baseline	Month 1	Month 2	Month 3	Previous Month
1. Number of long-form stories published	[#]	[#]	[#]	[#]	[#]
2. Number of social media posts published	[#]	[#]	[#]	[#]	[#]
3. Average views per long-form story	[#]	[#]	[#]	[#]	[#]
4. Number of client inquiries from stories	[#]	[#]	[#]	[#]	[#]
Total Kit Sales from Objective 1	[#]	[#]	[#]	[#]	[#]

Notes/Actions Taken

_____

_____

_____

_____

_____

_____

_____

_____

Objective 2: Drive 300 visitors to the Brand Kit sales pages in 90 days.

Key Result	Baseline	Month 1	Month 2	Month 3	Previous Month
1. Number of optimized blog posts	[#]	[#]	[#]	[#]	[#]
2. Visitors to Brand Kit pages	[#]	[#]	[#]	[#]	[#]
3. Average session duration on Brand Kit pages	[#]	[#]	[#]	[#]	[#]
4. Qualified leads generated from organic traffic	[#]	[#]	[#]	[#]	[#]
Total Kit Sales from Objective 2	[#]	[#]	[#]	[#]	[#]

Notes/Actions Taken

_____

_____

_____

_____

_____

_____

_____

_____

Objective 3: Boost engagement with Brand Kit content to support lead generation and sales.

Key Result	Baseline	Month 1	Month 2	Month 3	Previous Month
1. Number of high-engagement posts per week	[#]	[#]	[#]	[#]	[#]
2. New Instagram followers	[#]	[#]	[#]	[#]	[#]
3. New LinkedIn followers	[#]	[#]	[#]	[#]	[#]
4. Engagement rate per post (comments/shares)	[#]	[#]	[#]	[#]	[#]
Total Kit Sales from Objective 3	[#]	[#]	[#]	[#]	[#]

Notes/Actions Taken

_____

_____

_____

_____

_____

_____

_____

Summary of Results:

Key Result	Baseline	Month 1	Month 2	Month 3	Previous Month
1. Total Visitors to Kit Pages	[#]	[#]	[#]	[#]	[#]
2. Total Kit Sales (across all objectives)	[#]	[#]	[#]	[#]	[#]
3. Number of Leads Generated	[#]	[#]	[#]	[#]	[#]
4. Total Social Media Engagement (All Platforms)	[#]	[#]	[#]	[#]	[#]

Notes/Actions Taken

_____

_____

_____

_____

_____

_____

_____

_____

_____

_____

Additional Notes/Insights

Use this section to capture any qualitative insights, challenges, or learnings from the past month. Consider documenting any adjustments made to content strategy, SEO, or social media efforts based on performance.

_____

_____

Next Steps/Action Plan

This section should include a high-level outline of the actions you will take next month based on the insights gathered from this report.

_____

_____

Reporting Guide:

1. **Baseline**: Establish initial metrics for each key result at the start of the 90-day period.

2. **Monthly Tracking**: Input actual results for each key result on a monthly basis.

3. **Previous Month**: Include last month's performance for easy comparison.

4. **Notes/Actions Taken**: Record specific actions or strategic decisions taken that affected performance.

_____

_____

This template provides a clear structure for tracking and reporting on your OKRAs while offering space for reflection and strategic adjustments. You can easily expand this into a Google Sheet or Excel file for regular updates. And you can find this template at **https:// forgeandspark.com/content-with-purpose**

Helpful, yes?

Right out the gate, record your baseline metrics: the data recording where you're at for each key result right now. By doing so, you'll know exactly where you started from so that you can measure progress from this point forward.

If you haven't yet ensured that your key results are measurable and quantifiable within a specific time range, go back and do that now. This thinking will involve examining your Content Objectives and key results and considering what kinds of data points you want to see and can measure over time.

Here's a beautiful tip if you happen to be challenged, as I am, with the curse of being unable to think in data points and measurables: Use AI for this step, too.

My suggested prompt:

Given the following OKRs and actions/initiatives intended to meet this business objective [insert your business objective here], please revise to ensure that all key results are measurable on a monthly basis: [cut and paste your draft OKRs and actions here]

After this point, return to the prompt above to generate your Reporting Template and go to town measuring your success.

Oh, and don't forget to celebrate your wins! You'll have many, and celebrating yourself feels mighty good.

MESSAGING SPREADSHEET WORK

Now it's your turn. Give it a try below, or add your OKRAs to your spreadsheet.

Our Content Marketing Mission is to:

_____

_____

A Key Business Objective We're Working Toward

_____

_____

Content Objectives (Relating to Business Objective)

Objective 1:

_____

_____

Objective 2:

_____

_____

Objective 3:

_____

_____

Key Results

For Objective 1:

_____

_____

For Objective 2:

_____

_____

For Objective 3:

_____

_____

Actions/Initiatives

For Objective 1:

_____

_____

For Objective 2:

_____

_____

For Objective 3:

_____

_____

CHAPTER 6

UNDERSTANDING YOUR AUDIENCE

Once you've outlined and documented your Objectives and Key Results (OKRs), the next crucial step is identifying who can help you achieve them. Enter your target audience.

This is the next critical step in your messaging process: clarifying at least one target audience segment you want to market to, reach, or engage.

When it comes to messaging, your task will be getting to know and understand them so you can have a rich and productive conversation—ideally, help each other. As a content marketer, you will need to figure out the topics and messages that will be compelling to them and that they need to lean in, listen, be convinced, and ultimately take action. You'll also need to clarify what you eventually need them to do for you (and what will make them do that) to meet your objectives.

And because there's such a close relationship between your audience and your messaging, we've developed a framework for messaging that allows you to create them in tandem. I'll walk you through that in this chapter.

The Importance of Knowing Your Audience

Before we dive into the 'how' of audience development, let's revisit why it matters. Whether setting out to attract leads, encourage engagement, or drive sales, understanding your audience is the key to success.

Take a moment to review the OKRs you began developing in Chapter 4 (if you're following along). My hope is that at least one of your content marketing objectives is related to achieving measurable business results—whether that's attracting and engaging the right leads, leading some of your audience to explore an offer or service and get in touch, or perhaps promoting and selling a particular product or service.

To make traction on those objectives, a key question you'll need to answer in all those cases is: who are they specifically? What kinds of people are the suitable leads for your business? Who are they demographically, and what do they want and need from you? What problem are they looking to solve (relating to your content, products, or services)?

Knowing who will help you tactically when it comes to marketing and messaging. Having a particular audience in mind will, for example, enable you to conduct solid market or competitive research, targeted advertising, usability testing, and keyword research with specificity and efficiency.

Good personas are also vital to good messaging. A good persona will give you or your team insight into their needs and motivations that you can use to convey your message to the right audience at the right time. And if you're in a values-led business that needs to educate your customers and build trust, you must understand who you're talking to and what they need and want from you so that you can both 'speak their language' and cater to their needs.

Benefits of Knowing Your Audience

When you know your audience well, you can:

- **Create Personalized Content:** Tailor content that feels like a one-on-one conversation, making it more relatable and engaging.

- **Deliver Relevant Messaging:** Serve the right message at the right time, directly addressing your audience's challenges.

- **Optimize Content Strategy:** Focus your efforts on what matters to your audience, which will lead to more meaningful connections and conversions.

- **Enhance Content Promotion:** Promote your content using the most effective channels (e.g., social media and newsletters) where your audience is most active.

- **Develop Targeted Ads:** Build precise ad personas for platforms like Google or Facebook to ensure your advertising reaches the right people.

- **Improve SEO:** Use audience insights to identify the keywords and phrases your audience is searching for, boosting organic traffic and lead generation.

How to Create an Audience Persona for Your Content Marketing: An Overview

As we'll discover over the following few chapters, good content marketing depends on understanding your audience so that you can reach and engage them effectively. Throughout the book, I'll guide you through the process of creating a compelling audience persona. This section offers a high-level overview of how you'll do it. And here's a template you can fill in along the way, using our model of creating a content value proposition for your audience.

SHORT DESCRIPTION OF PERSONA OR ROLE *(High-level description of this audience)*		

JOBS TO BE DONE	PAINS	CONTENT GAINS
What does this persona need to get done, functionally or emotionally?	What pains or challenges are they looking to address (with your help)?	How might your content help to drive action or alleviate pain points?

ACTIONS TO PROMPT	TOPICS TO APPEAL	KINDS OF CONTENT
What specific action do you want them to take as a result of your content?	What core topics will meet your needs and theirs?	What channels, formats will work best for you and them?

Remember: you can find all templates at
https://forgeandspark.com/content-with-purpose

1. Gather the Basics: Your Audience's Demographics & Behaviour

Start with the basics. Record what you know about your target audience's demos, including their age, gender, income, education, and location—as relevant to your brand or business. These primary identifiers help you understand your audience at a surface level and can enable you to place them within a broader market context. Knowing this stuff is also very handy for targeted advertising later.

You can use tools like Google Analytics, social media insights, or email marketing platforms here to give you the skinny and understand how your audience behaves online. What content do they engage most and least with? Which social platforms do they frequent or avoid? Understanding their behaviour reveals how they interact with your brand and content—critical for shaping a strategy that fits their habits.

2. Get to Know 'Em: Psychographic Insights

This is the fun stuff: human psychology. Psychographic factors will help you understand what motivates, delights, and worries your audience. These factors include their interests, values, attitudes, and lifestyle choices, as well as their dislikes, fears, and no-go zones. This is the part about understanding your audience as a group of very human individuals with specific motivations so that you can gain insight and empathy.

3. Ask 'Em: Direct Contact With Your Audience

Move from the unknown to the understood by having conversations with your customers. You can—and should—conduct surveys, interviews, or informal chats with your existing customers or target audience, asking thoughtful questions that reveal their needs, challenges, goals, and preferences related to your products or services. This process can be transformational for many business owners and marketers, giving you direct insights that will guide you in crafting messages that feel like they're written for them, not at them.

A key thing to remember here as you ask all the good questions is 'message mining', which I'll outline further below. You can gain a deep understanding of your audience's needs and preferences—in their own words—which you can then use in your messaging to convey your empathy and understanding. Remember that you'll need to survey the places where your audience is communicating (or ask them directly) to gain insight into how they're expressing their challenges, needs, and desired solutions. It's a data-driven way to help you come up with not only an understanding of your audience but also, often, the words and phrasing that will most resonate with them as they seek and find your solutions.

4. Begin to Identify Their 'Jobs,' Pain Points, and Aspirations

To create content that drives action, you need to know what keeps your audience up at night and what they're striving for. We'll walk you through our process in this book for identifying and clarifying their jobs to be done, pain points, and gain points—encapsulating what they're trying to accomplish, the problems they're trying to solve, and the ways you can most help them, with your products, services, and content. These critical insights will enable you to tailor your content to directly and empathetically address their needs, offering personalized value that leads to trust and engagement.

5. Draft Your Target Personas

With all this data and insight in hand (and even before), I encourage you to draft at least one representative profile of the kind of audience member or customer you most want and need ... you guessed it ... to help you accomplish your content and business objectives. Let your inner author shine, giving this persona a name, a background, and specific attributes that encapsulate their traits and behaviours (like their jobs to be done, challenges, and pain points) and the kinds of benefits they're looking for your products, services, and content to deliver for them. These personas become the foundation for all your content marketing efforts, serving as a human blueprint for every piece of content you create.

6. Validate and Evolve Your Personas

Consider any documented persona you create as a living document—not set in stone. As you gather more data and insights, continually validate and refine them. We update ours continually, knowing that customer behaviour changes, new platforms and channels for publishing emerge, and your business will likely adapt and evolve over time to keep up. You'll learn more about your customers as you grow, including how they speak, seek out services like yours, and what they most love and hate about your content. Take good notes.

Who Should Be a Persona & How to Define Your Audience

Building meaningful relationships with your audience starts with understanding who they are. If you haven't developed audience personas yet, don't worry—this is an ongoing discovery process, and you're about to start.

Envision Your Ideal Audience

If you don't already have sales, customer segments, or personas for your organization, a great place to begin is to envision one customer, client, audience member, or group you'd love to serve—and who will serve your business, too. Review your key business objective and OKRs now. Keeping them in mind, ask: What kind of audience, client, or customer does my business need to ensure I reach that objective? This is about starting with an audience group or a particular client whom you love and want more of and considering what they want or need from your business and your content. And don't worry if you're unclear yet. Just begin by keeping the end in mind.

Dig Into Your Data to See Who's in Your Audience Now (And Who You're Missing)

Find out what you can from your data: Google Analytics, social media insights and reporting, and email marketing. Who's reading your stuff? Who's visiting and leaving right away? Who's clicking or opening? What are they consuming, liking, and commenting on most and least? Make a list. Put it in a spreadsheet. And psst: If you don't already know your targeted audience actions, looking at data and identifying what you get most excited about seeing is your clue!

Talk to Your Teams

What results (or lack thereof) is your sales team most focused on? Your marketing team? Who among your online audience do they feel is most and least important to your business bottom line? What audience actions are they most jazzed about?

Get to Know the Competition (And Who They're Talking To)

Don't be shy about checking out your competitors' sites and social channels when identifying your potential audience segments or personas. Dig into the feeds of your best and fiercest competitors to find out who they're talking to and how they're serving them with content. Make a note of how they speak to these folks on their websites. Always observe the messaging that underlies their content: What are they saying to their followers and customers beneath the copy? Then note what you love and what you could do with your resources, and consider 'stealing like an artist,' as AUSTIN KLEON says. Or like an excellent marketer.

Speak Directly to Potential Personas

When I launched Forge & Spark in 2012, I had no idea what I was doing or who I wanted to serve. I quickly learned, through trial and error, who I did—and didn't—enjoy working with. However, I didn't clearly understand what value I provided or what those enjoyable clients most needed from me. So I asked. And they answered! Most customers don't mind offering their opinions if they know why you're asking and if they feel like you're honouring and appreciating their generosity. So ask.

At our agency, we sometimes tack on a couple of questions to the end of a Zoom call or send out a quick survey explaining how their answers will help us. Be patient, and express your gratitude. It works. You can gain a deep understanding of what your ideal audience is looking for and how they have experienced their time working with you. This information is invaluable and can help guide your future objectives, key results, and actions.

Gaining Audience Insight: What to Ask Your Potential Personas

At Forge & Spark, we've developed and shared our list of tried-and-true persona questions, listed in the table below, which roughly divide into questions about your audience's motivations (or 'Jobs to be Done'), their demographics, a few more deep dive questions depending on whether they're on the B2C or B2B side, and some questions to disqualify customers, too.

Just as important as knowing who you want your audience to be, though, is understanding who you don't want to serve, so included as well is a section on 'negative' audience information.

When you set up a call or survey with your audience, save some time by starting with these tried-and-true questions to understand better what they most need and want from you. Armed with answers, you'll be able to start sketching out informed and human personas for your marketing. Most importantly, you'll have a person in mind when you develop messaging that drives results.

Questions to Ask for Better Messaging

DEMOGRAPHICS

1. What is your customer's age?

2. What gender do they identify with, if any?

3. Do they have children? If so, how many and what are their ages?

4. What is their marital status?

5. Where do they live?

6. What is their personal or household income?

7. What is their education level?

PROFESSIONAL DETAILS FOR B2B

1. Where does your customer work?

2. What is their job title and/or primary role?

3. What's their career path like?

4. What industry do they work in?

5. How big is the company they work for?

6. How would they describe their typical day?

7. What special skills do they have?

8. What tools do they use to do their job?

9. Who is their boss, and what is their relationship like?

10. Do they manage others?

11. How is their success measured?

MOTIVATIONS: GOALS AND CHALLENGES

1. What personal and/or career goals does this buyer have?

2. How do they prioritize them?

3. What challenges impact their ability to achieve these goals?

4. What problems does this cause for them?

5. How could your products or services help with those challenges?

6. What would prompt them to seek a solution?

MOTIVATIONS: VALUES AND FEARS

1. What do they value in their personal or professional life?

2. What's important to them when considering a product like yours?

3. What objections might they have to making the purchase?

4. What drives their decision-making process?

5. Which competitors (if any) might they consider?

6. What would happen if they picked the wrong solution?

7. What would happen if they did nothing at all?

BEHAVIOUR AND HABITS

1. How does your buyer get information?

2. How do they communicate?

3. What media do they consume?

4. Do they belong to any associations?

5. What social media do they use?

6. Do they attend events or conferences? If so, which ones?

7. Where do they spend their days?

8. Do they have any relevant hobbies?

NEGATIVE PERSONA INFORMATION: WHO YOU DON'T WANT

1. Which types of customers are too difficult or expensive to support?

2. Are there certain customers who don't have the budget for what you offer?

3. Is your product a bad fit or simply not designed for certain industries or individuals?

Gaining Further Audience Insight: Message Mining

When it comes to crafting your own messaging statements, start by listening. What are your customers, audience members, or clients saying—both *about* you and *to* you? And what actual words and phrases are they using? This is where message mining comes in. Message mining is simply listening to what your audience and customers are saying about you, and capturing those sentiments, phrases, and words for use in your own messaging, marketing, and content.

Mining words and phrases from reviews of our services and paying close attention to how people talk about our brand in social comments and DM questions can be a truly excellent way to observe how others perceive your brand. And directly asking is key. With new leads, for example, I ask this as part of a standard First Discovery call: "I'm curious about what led you to get in touch. What are some of the main things you took away from our website and social channels when you checked us out?" I also record those calls (with permission), and make note in my own messaging documentation about particular phrases, words, and ideas they shared. This process informs my own copywriting and content creation, and often gives me great ideas for future articles and posts, too.

I apply message mining not only to reading reviews, but to my conversations with leads and existing clients, too. For example, I ask— as a part of our annual Health Check-In with clients, or when it arises naturally in more periodic check-ins, whether they follow any of our social or blog content, what they think of it, and what they think it's saying about us. I usually record their responses and make careful note of the words and phrases they use to describe us.

And don't forget just paying attention to what people out there are saying about you in comments on social posts, in reviews (on Google, Yelp, or industry-specific sites like Clutch, or others), or in DMs or emails they send to you or your general company inbox.

Any way you do it, you will be bound to discover some surprisingly helpful and valuable anecdotal evidence from an audience you care about, showing you how your brand messaging (and content) is landing for your audience and how they perceive you as a brand. Such insight can be helpful in adjusting or trying out new phrasing or messaging in your content so that you may find ways to better connect with future clients, too.

With messaging mining, you'll not only better understand your target audience but also create content that speaks directly to them. The key here is to listen carefully not only to the substance of what they're saying, but also how they're saying it.

How to Use Message Mining in Your Marketing

In my experience, message mining can be used to develop a content marketing strategy, messaging strategy, positioning research, and copywriting. It can also help develop your website, landing page, or ad copy.Message mining interviews are also very closely aligned with the jobs-to-be-done framework, which we'll be using in developing your content value proposition. This approach generally asks you to directly interview your customers or audience to discover—in their own words— what they most need from your products, services, or content.

Here's an outline of how you might consider using this technique.

1. Start by clarifying the outcomes you're hoping for from message mining: This approach is a great help in extracting valuable insights and meaningful patterns from the messages your customers and audiences are sending to you so that you can better understand them and speak to them in their language. Your first step is determining whether this is a priority in your marketing.

2. Consider what's most important to capture: What kind of information are you most looking to uncover or analyze? As someone who tends to follow rabbit holes and shiny objects, firmly identifying my objectives is always helpful in saving a lot of time down the line. Studying what people say about you can take you in a thousand different directions. Focus on what matters most now and take notes for later.

3. Identify your most relevant data sources: Where are the best places to find the messages you want to mine? Some great starting points include conversations or DMs on your social channels, sales platforms, or chatbots; actual conversations recorded with your leads or clients; emails or questions that come in from your website contact forms; and testimonials from your clients or transcriptions of calls you've had with clients.

4. Gather all the beautiful (and not-so-beautiful) messages: Collect the messaging that genuinely represents your audiences. It should represent each of your audience segments or customer personas and be diverse enough to provide comprehensive insights.

5. Clean up your data: Review and organize the messages to eliminate noise and indicate priority. You don't have to keep them all. Fix any typos and severe grammatical issues—being careful not to lose the essence of the phrasing—and get rid of any inconsistent messages. You'll feel relief.

6. Discuss what you uncover: Take the time with your team—anyone involved in sales, marketing, and content creation—to review and make sense of the mined messages you've gathered. Your goal here is to gain insight into your audience and possible messaging and copy that you can apply in your content marketing and messaging.

7. Gather and communicate your insights and conclusions: This exercise will undoubtedly teach you valuable things about your audiences and what they need from you. This is handy stuff! Capture it in a way that you'll use. I suggest adding your insights to your roadmap or communication guidelines or adding the highlights to your messaging framework. However you do it, ensure that your takeaways are communicated so that they can make a real difference to your marketing.

Message mining is a fairly simple process that helps you understand what your target market wants and how they talk about their pains, needs, and situations. You can use that information to inform your actual copy and the way you market your products and services.

And it's not likely something you'll do just once and never again; once you go through the exercise, you'll likely have it on your mind. I suggest working it into your strategic process and refreshing your findings often. Doing so will help you gain valuable knowledge about connecting with the people who matter most to your business.

Understanding the Customer Journey and Speaking to It

In my agency, we strategically use buyer personas to guide the development of specific messaging for each customer journey stage. This strategy ensures we reach our audience with the most relevant content and messaging at the ideal time to 'nudge' them closer to helping us achieve our objectives.

Broadly, we think about these stages as follows:

Discovery & Awareness

Stage Goal: Acquire new audiences by attracting brand attention and growing views and follows.

Kinds of Content: High-Level Content to Capture Attention, which appeals to values, answers questions, and captivates visually.

Typical Formats:

- Short videos (e.g., Reels, TikToks, YouTube Shorts)
- SEO-optimized blogs
- Infographics
- Short info-bites

Engagement

Stage Goal: Engage audiences by getting people interested in your brand, so they're inclined to do business with you.

Kinds of Content: Lightly Branded Content that highlights the brand's unique value and values, making people curious to learn more.

Typical Formats:

- Interactive content, such as event coverage and events
- Newsletters
- Informative social media stories/posts
- Podcasts
- Personal engagement with content

Consideration & Conversion

Stage Goal: Compel targeted action by offering content that leads to a decision.

Kinds of Content: Branded Content that allows people to learn more and dive deeper so they can evaluate the brand as a valuable option. Your website should be the main source for this content, with social content driving audiences there.

Typical Formats:

- Case studies and success stories
- Demos, tutorials, and guides
- Courses
- Testimonials and reviews
- Informative website copy

Trust, Loyalty, & Advocacy

Stage Goal: Retain audiences and ensure they want to stay.

Kinds of Content: Human & Values-Rich Content, which appreciates people and creates or reflects a valued relationship. This content should prompt emotion and foster a human connection.

Typical Formats:

- Member stories and profiles

- Member testimonials and quotes

- Community engagement initiatives

- "VIP" offers and exclusive content

- Consistent updates and follow-ups

- Thought leadership content, such as opinion pieces, articles, and research

Another model commonly used to describe content used in the marketing 'funnel' is the top (TOFU), Middle (MOFU), and Bottom (BOFU) of Funnel content.

Whatever model you use, the logic is essentially the same: to drive a targeted action—whether that's buying your thing, signing up for a list, or giving you a phone call—you first need to make sure that person is a) aware of who you are and what you offer; and b) gets to a point (most often thanks to information, education, trust-building, and relationship-building) where they're ready to take action.

Applying Your Audience Knowledge: Key Approaches

We've seen that audience research can and should include analysing data, monitoring comments and conversations, conducting competitive research, and direct conversation—among other methods. But even if you don't know everything you need to about your audience, you can begin 'filling in the blanks' to craft useful personas

Previously, I've mentioned that a good starting point for developing empathetic personas for your brand or business is to start with one audience group—or even a specific customer or client—in mind and mentally get into their headspace.

It might sound basic, but it works. I come from a creative writing background and think of this exercise as the fun part of messaging development. It's where you get to see the world from your main character's point of view and begin to paint a picture of how they perceive it. The customer should, after all, be the protagonist in the story you're telling them—or rather, the hero in the Hero's Journey.

Considering Your Customer's 'Hero Journey'

Donald Miller's StoryBrand Framework provides another way to consider the customer journey and helps craft narrative messaging that speaks to that journey. I highly recommend checking out his book.

His approach is grounded in deeply understanding your customers' (or audiences') key challenges or pain points and knowing where they need to be at the journey's end, both emotionally *and* practically. It's all about positioning your brand—or **you,** if you're a consultant or direct service provider—as the 'guide.'

Think of yourself or your brand as the Yoda to your client's Luke in Star Wars. The Morpheus to their Neo. The Dumbledore to their Harry Potter.

For Miller, StoryBrand messaging is all about telling your audience a story about how you can serve as that kind of guide and what you can ultimately do for them ... spelling out, along the way, the perils of NOT choosing you and what it will cost them. His framework involves developing specific messaging that communicates how you, as a guide, can help your customer solve the problem and reap fabulous benefits, then communicating that message through a narrative story structure.

This can be remarkably compelling to story-trained audiences (like me) and also proves an eye-opening exercise for owners and marketers.

In my professional experience, however, the hero's journey approach can sometimes leave leaders and marketers scratching their heads regarding exactly how to apply that hero's journey story in 'regular marketing,' including daily social media posts, for example, and specific campaigns. Do you, for example, tell the whole story at once? Do you have to say to it over time? How can you make it make sense in a single X post?

It's a tricky approach to use in all businesses, too—technology offerings and complex service businesses, for example, have had a hard time putting what sometimes feels like an overly simplistic story arc to work for them. And it can, if executed poorly, also sound cheesy or overblown. Still, it can prove a worthwhile addition to your messaging mix and is a fun story to develop if you're a creative writer like me. It also works powerfully for numerous businesses and service types.

Here's my summary of the seven-step process—but again, it's worthwhile to go to the source and buy Miller's book and training.

- **Identify the customer's problem:** Define the problem your customer is facing and how your brand can help solve it.

- **Position your brand as the guide:** Position your brand as the guide who can help the customer solve their problem.

- **Create a clear message:** Develop a clear and concise message that communicates how your brand can help the customer solve their problem.

- **Use a story structure:** Use a story structure to create a narrative that engages the customer and helps them see how your brand fits into their story.

- **Make the customer the hero:** Position the customer as the story's hero and your brand as the guide who helps them achieve their goals.

- **Create a plan:** Develop a plan that outlines the steps the customer needs to take to achieve their goals with your brand's help.

- **Call to action:** End with a clear call to action that encourages the customer to take action and engage with your brand.

The Value Proposition Approach

For businesses that want to go beyond the hero's journey, creating messaging that speaks to their offerings and values and addresses specific customer needs, we've adapted the seriously brilliant Strategyzer model for use in not just product development (for which it was initially developed) but also content marketing.

This model is, in fact, at the heart of our approach to developing empathetic strategy that achieves that elusive message-market match, or resonance, introduced in Chapter 1. It balances an understanding of your audience's needs with your own as a business or brand, to deliver a clear picture of the messaging you need to serve both sides. See? Brilliant.

The Strategyzer Model

The Strategyzer Value Proposition Canvas, developed by Alex Osterwalder, Yves Pigneur, Greg Bernardo, and Alan Smith, is a tool initially designed to help businesses define (and refine) the unique value that their product or service provides to customers—what they call their *value proposition*.

Noting that this was designed as a tool to help businesses define and refine their products and services, the gist is that you develop your products and services to meet the needs of your audience.

Why not use it as a communication tool and consider how your content can directly address your customers' needs and pain points while informing them about your products and services?

How it Works for Products & Services

The model is divided into two sections: the customer profile and the value map.

The customer profile section is where you can get familiar with what's in your customers' heads and hearts by identifying their needs, pains, and gains. **Needs** are the things that customers require to achieve their goals, **pains** are the things that frustrate or hinder them, and **gains** are the benefits they hope to achieve.

The value map section is where you as a business can better clarify how your offerings—your products or services—address precisely those customer needs, pains, and gains you've identified. **Products and services** are the features and benefits of the product or service, **pain relievers** are how the product or service addresses customer pains, and **gain creators** are how the product or service creates value for customers.

It's a valuable exercise for gaining a deeper understanding of where your customers are coming from when they're looking for help from your products or services and for getting to the nitty-gritty of exactly how you can serve them. It also frequently highlights areas where your products or services are not quite filling their needs. So, from a product development standpoint, it's an invaluable tool for refining products or services and developing new products that can better meet customers where they're at.

Adapting the Value Proposition Model to Content Marketing

From my perspective as a communicator, the Value Proposition model can also serve as an excellent tool for helping to develop and optimize messaging and creating the kinds of content that will lead audiences to learn about, engage with, and ultimately consider buying your offering.

Therefore, the framework we've developed for messaging at Forge & Spark is tuned to content first: rather than using the tool to improve businesses' offerings, we use it—with a few modifications—to zero in on what to say and how to say it to encourage an audience to meet those OKRs we've been talking about. Let's get into that next.

CHAPTER 7

WORKING YOUR MESSAGING MAP

Now that you understand the foundational pieces for your messaging, rooted in your business and content goals and your audience (who you'll most need to reach, engage, and speak with to achieve those goals), it's time to put it all on virtual paper. This chapter will introduce you to the Messaging Map we use at Forge & Spark to clarify your audience's content jobs, pains, and gains—and how we apply that understanding to define messages that you and your team can actively use.

Our framework is kind of a four-fer. By completing a straightforward spreadsheet (which we call the Messaging Map), you'll have a document that gathers—all in one place—your clarified OKRs; your most important personas; your most important messaging for those personas; and a collection of brilliant ideas for the kinds of content that's going to work best to reach and engage those personas at the various stages of their customer journey—messaging that will make them know, feel, and believe what you'd most like them to.

Let's now take a look at developing your Messaging Map. Below, I've outlined the core elements that you'll include.

You're welcome to set up your spreadsheet in Google Sheets or Excel using the outline below, or you may access any of our templates, outlined in the Resource section of this book and available for download at: **https://forgeandspark.com/content-with-purpose.**

Your Messaging Map Spreadsheet

The Audience-Based Messaging Map is a strategic tool designed to guide you to consider, clarify, and then craft a number of clear, compelling messages that articulate a brand's value proposition in a way that resonates with a specific target audience.

Full Messaging is divided into four sections: Audience Focus, *You* Focus, Stage-Based Messaging, and Content Capture, which I will describe in full below. Please note that I've also provided a Simplified Messaging sheet in the downloadable Messaging Map, which omits Stage-Based Messaging.

Audience Focus

For every persona you've created, your Messaging Map outlines their 'job to be done' (what they need to accomplish), their pain points, and the potential gains that your content might provide them—all based on your empathetic understanding of their jobs to be done and pain points. This section of the map helps you see the world from your audience's perspective, in order to guide your messaging and marketing efforts.

AUDIENCE FOCUS		
THEIR "JOB TO BE DONE"	PAINS	GAINS
What this audience wants/ needs to get done. Includes functional tasks, social jobs, or the emotional state they want to achieve.	Pains you can help to alleviate. Might include negative emotions, undesired costs or situations, risks.	How might your offering or your content genuinely help or benefit them?

You Focus

Again for each persona, your Messaging Map then delves into the action you want to prompt with your messaging or content, and what that persona needs to **know**, **feel**, and **believe** in order to take the desired action. This section of the map enables you and your marketing team to clarify what you need your audience to do, and the logical and emotional messaging that should underpin all of your content in order to drive that action.

YOU FOCUS	
THE ACTION YOU NEED TO PROMPT	KNOW, FEEL, BELIEVE
What specific action do you want them to take as a result of your messaging?	What does your audience need to know or understand, feel, and believe, in order to prompt that desired action?

Stage-Based Messaging

The next section of the map is helpful for anyone looking to create messaging to nudge their audience along a journey from awareness to action. It's broken down into stages of the buyer's journey—TOFU (Top of the Funnel), MOFU (Middle of the Funnel), and BOFU (Bottom of the Funnel)—helping you tailor your messaging according to where your audience is in their decision-making process.

STAGE-BASED MESSAGING		
TOP OF FUNNEL (TOFU)	MID-FUNNEL (MOFU)	BOTTOM OF FUNNEL (BOFU)
What content or message might catch this persona's attention at a high level?	What might pique this persona's interest in your brand's knowledge or services?	What content or message could convince them to take a targeted action or buy from you?

Stage-Based Messaging

Finally, Map presents you with a helpful 'parking lot' for content ideas and additional messaging to further differentiate your brand and address specific needs.

CONTENT CAPTURE	
KEY CONTENT IDEAS	**ADDITIONAL MESSAGING**
Capture any content ideas to help to drive action for this specific persona.	What else might you say to let this group know you're better than the rest? Additional notes welcome.

Overall, the map is designed to ensure that your messaging effectively addresses your audience's unique needs and desires at every stage of their journey, while keeping your own marketing requirements top of mind, where they belong. It's a simple tool for crafting resonant messaging that ultimately drives action.

Where to Start: Your Most Important Audience Group

Start with your best or ideal audience. I like to start messaging by imagining my most important client: the one I'd like to replicate a few times over. Then, I'll ask them for a little of their time or send them a survey that asks the questions that we'll answer in this spreadsheet. People are surprisingly willing to take 10-15 minutes to help you when they get to talk about themselves a little. Plus, you're very likely to get a testimonial or more work out of the exercise. Go on, try it!

Have you got your person? Great. Name them something you'll remember that feels right. For years, we've called our ideal client Lovely Lucy. This persona is based on an actual client who was a pure pleasure to work with. She appreciated our emphasis on quality, she shared and respected our values, she always valued our expertise and paid us what we were worth (and on time), she grew her business into a certified B

Corp, and was generally fantastic. You can see why we wanted to get in her head and work with more people like her.

Again, here's our complete persona. You don't have to worry about developing this quite yet—it will come after you finish filling in your spreadsheet—but I'll share it here for reference.

JOBS TO BE DONE	PAINS	GAINS	CONTENT
Generate clear business value from marketing efforts Feel proud of consistently impressive content and marketing Take content marketing OFF their to-do list (while ensuring her high standards are met)	Waaay too much on their plate! Business growing pains: new opportunities & products require new marketing strategies Feels behind / unprepared / unskilled in content marketing and/or strategy (it's not their wheelhouse) Embarrassed & frustrated by their brand content (or lack thereof)	Thoughtful, premium-quality content impresses their audience and makes them look savvy & smart Clear business results and content aligned with brand purpose & values Their team is learning from us and is able to strategize/create content more effectively They love working with a thoroughly professional (and fun!) team that can be trusted	Impress them by demonstrating our expertise and experience Delight them with its originality, warmth, and effectiveness Inspire trust that we are knowledgeable, experienced experts Prompt them to learn more about us and our offerings and reach out (email to book a call)

Jobs To Be Done

We've mentioned jobs to be done (JTBD) a few times now, and it's time to get into it. Determining your audience's jobs to be done can be tricky—but I'd advise you to keep it simple and common sense. Simply ask yourself this fundamental question: As it relates to what your business offers, what are the actual 'jobs' (think: functional tasks, social jobs, and the emotional state they want to achieve ultimately) that they're trying to get done?

And while the questions seem simple, there's a lot to unpack.

First, What IS a 'Job'?

It all started with a theory in the 1990s put forward by Clayton Christensen and a group of his colleagues at Harvard Business School.

The theory aims to understand and address customers' needs by focusing on the 'jobs' they are trying to accomplish. The central idea is that consumers 'hire' products or services to perform specific tasks or jobs. Such jobs might be purely functional—like quenching one's thirst—or emotional—like feeling pup. When marketing a new beverage, you can see that understanding the underlying motivation behind a customer's decision-making process is critical to producing and marketing just the right product.

Identifying these jobs can be accomplished by delving into a group of customers' behaviours, goals, frustrations, and aspirations—all to better understand the context in which customers buy. This theory was initially developed to help businesses uncover unmet needs and design solutions that align with customers' desired outcomes. But we have also applied it successfully in marketing.

It represents a departure from the demographic-centric personas or customer avatars you might use. Applied to content marketing, the JTBD framework asks us to look at what 'job' our audiences need to do when they approach our marketing content.

Do they, for example, just need to decide which product to choose? Are they looking to get more informed? Do they just want to figure out how the damned product works and how they can use it to benefit their life?

Understanding these fundamental jobs can help us as marketers create content that prompts them to learn more, trust us, and do business with us.

The Difference Between Jobs and Needs

One key thing to understand as you tackle your customers' JTBD is that, according to this theory, a 'job' is different from a 'need.' Here are a few examples based on marketing a product for sale.

An alarm clock

While your customer may need an alarm clock, their actual 'job to be done' is to wake up on time.

A drill

> *"People don't want a quarter-inch drill. They want a quarter-inch hole."*
>
> Theodore Levitt

This well-known quote perfectly illustrates a job to be done, where the customer's job is to drill the correct-sized hole in their wall. They might need a drill to do it, but ultimately, they have a specific need. Going even deeper, we might also discover more jobs. They might, for example, want to hang a heavy picture. Or to enhance the appearance of their room. Ultimately, they might just want to feel less like a broke college student and have some impressive art on their walls. Can you see how knowing these different tasks and desired feelings can help you immensely as you set out to develop different messages to reach and engage this consumer?

A coffee maker

You want to sell a coffee maker to a specific person. What's their functional job? What feeling do they want to have after engaging with your content or buying the coffee maker?

Here, you can see that what you get is going to be very different for very different audiences. While one person just wants to get one cup of decent coffee into their body as quickly as possible (get this person a single-serve maker, stat!), another might care deeply about drinking only the best quality coffee (top-of-the-line espresso maker here, please).

You might also figure out, as we did with a client, that an audience's JTBD was mixed. Their audience wanted good coffee that was sustainably produced but didn't care so much about top-of-the-line quality. For them, it was a matter of finding the right ground to stand on: making it clear that they were getting quality without needing to feel snobby or entitled and that they were not disregarding sustainability was the fine line we walked.

A Trick: Consider a Person's Multitudes

Walt Whitman reminded us that we each contain multitudes. Your audience does, too. One way to drill down to a persona's JTBDs while also getting into their heads and hearts is to try to see things from their perspectives.

I'm a business owner. But I'm also a marketer who tries to be true to my value of showing up authentically. I'm also a busy mom with limited time. I also occasionally rock out with my band, Hot Flash. And so on.

Each of these roles can affect what I want and need from a brand, depending which 'hat' I may be wearing, and what my mindset is, or needs are, at a given moment..

Try asking yourself what your audience's jobs are from a few standpoints. I suggest starting with Human Person, Specific Role(s), and Brand Representative.

Do I contradict myself?
Very well then,
I contradict myself.
(I am large, I contain multitudes.)

—WALT WHITMAN, SONG OF MYSELF

Forge & Spark Example

To initially develop our agency's primary persona, Lucy, we interviewed one of our favourite clients. We asked them the questions posed in your Messaging Map: their pain points, what led them to reach out to us, what they were most hoping to solve, what kinds of gains they wanted to emerge with from an engagement with an agency like ours, and what they wanted to know, feel, and believe, to make a decision.

From those answers, combined with our experience with clients similar to Lucy, we were able to draft a Persona we could use in our sales and marketing. We also learned a hell of a lot about Lucy's real motivations and needs and about what she valued most (and least) about us. It was an incredibly valuable exercise that we integrated into our customer service and marketing processes.

We've workshopped our Lucy persona over the years since, and have created and iterated on a suite of other client personas using the same kind of process.

Lucy is a representative example of C-suite leaders and decision-makers in purpose-led businesses. **As a human,** their 'job' is to publish content they feel genuinely proud of, and that occasionally prompts friends and respected colleagues (or competitors) to reach out with compliments. This content has to look top-notch, represents their brand values, and has integrity. And hoo boy, as a human, they also desperately want more free time—which means they need to be able to trust somebody else to steer the content marketing ship. Our Lucys are busy folks. **As a business owners or leader,** they're always conscious of the bottom line. And **as someone who leads marketing for the brand,** they (or their small team) rarely have the time to be able to 'do content' at the level of quality they know is required. Finally, **as a representative of their brand,** a top priority is 'showing up' in marketing and sales materials with integrity—and without the sales-schmoozy factor she and her customers despise.

You can see from this example (and you may know quite well yourself) that one persona can have a whole lot of jobs. It's your job, next, to sort out which jobs your messaging and content can best address.

For our Lucy, we prioritized the following Jobs To Be Done:

- Generate clear business value from marketing efforts

- Feel proud of consistently impressive content and marketing

- Take content marketing OFF their to-do list (while ensuring her high standards are met

YOUR TURN

Ready to give it a try yourself? Consider the audience group or persona you identified in the first step. Without overthinking, take a moment and answer the following questions as they relate to your offerings and content:

- *What functional tasks are they trying to accomplish? What actual tasks might they get done by reading/consuming your stuff?*

- *What emotional tasks are they looking to fulfil? How do they want to feel due to using a product or service like yours or consuming your content?*

- *When it comes to your content, what are they looking to accomplish or feel as a human, as a representative of their marketing role, or as a representative of their brand?*

Pains

Getting clear on your audience's pain points is often a matter of research, gathering data, and directly asking people to share. This is a must. But most likely, you can make a pretty good guess.

As a business owner and someone who's almost always on early discovery calls with clients who have been referred to me or who have found my business online, I hear pain points about content marketing all the time. Things like:

- My team is 'doing' content, but I'm not sure we're accomplishing anything.

- Our content is off-brand and doesn't sound like us.

- I don't have enough time to do all this content marketing! Help!

- I don't think we have enough knowledge or skills to do social media marketing right.

- There's no way I can keep up with tools/trends/best practices in SEO, social media etc.

This doesn't cover the gamut of every client's pain points, but such notes are precisely the notes I'd document in my spreadsheet to remind myself and inform my team about the real struggles—in the clients' own words—that our clients face. This shared understanding enables us to then develop content, products, and services to support these folks, and prospective clients like them.

And Don't Forget Broader Objections

Another way to consider your customer's pain points is to go one step further, noting their possible objections to buying from you. What is the simplest way to do this? Consider the top two or three questions people always ask about your product or service when you pitch or sell—and the possible objections behind those questions. People ask questions because they want answers about things they care about. Their questions show their areas of care and concern.

We are almost always asked about two things: cost and time. These are crucial considerations for service providers and consultants because they are at the top of anyone's mind when they consider you.

The questions we get about time are multiple. How long does it take to develop a strategy? How much of a leader's time is required? How much would they personally (and their teams) have to invest in the process of reviewing and approving content every month? What they're asking is: *How much of a pain in the ass will this be more me and my team? And can I afford to take that time out of my busy schedule?*

Regarding cost, it's a little more straightforward. How much for the project or the retainer? How does the pricing work for strategy vs. ongoing content support? Is there a discount for non-profits? The subtext there is essential, though: *Tell me the number so that I can compare it to the alternative, which is, for us, hiring someone internally, finding a less expensive agency, or doing nothing at all.*

I hope you can see from this simple example how important it is to understand your audience's pain points and objections and address them in your messaging. Sometimes, you have to learn this the hard way: Before addressing these objections in our messaging and web copy, we lost many clients to cheaper agencies and couldn't even count how many leads we lost due to the uncertainty about both cost and time required. Thankfully, our framework helped us address them.

As a business owner, Lucy faces some common struggles when it comes to marketing. Almost always, our qualified CEO leads approach us with a variation of: *I'm overwhelmed and feel like we have no strategy when it comes to marketing.* What it boils down to, when we do further investigation, are these four pain points:

Limited time / way too much on their plates

Lucy has to get their marketing team (or themself) to get content out in the world, to tell their audience about their company and products or services. They usually do it by the seat of their pants, ad hoc or daily. And it almost always takes way more time than they bargained for to ideate, create, edit, format, and publish content, so they're always behind.

Business growing pains / can't keep up: New opportunities & products require new marketing strategies

Our Lucys tell us that even if they go ahead with 'regular content marketing'—there's always something else to strategize, plan, or talk about. Lucy wonders how to keep up with the basic messaging when there's an urgent need to sell something new.

Feels "not the best at" content marketing and strategy

Lucy and her team are doing their best, but they see that the content isn't always doing what they want it to (lack of strategy). And Lucy feels like they're 'throwing spaghetti against the wall' to see what works.

Embarrassed and frustrated by their content (or lack thereof)

These anxieties can weigh heavily on business owners, sapping our confidence. When considering your personas' pain points, then, remember that emotions and fears often drive action more effectively than logic. Your content should aim to acknowledge and address these deeper concerns.

What about *your* audience? What kinds of challenges do they have that your product or service can address—and more to the point for content marketing—that your content might help to address?

> HOT TIP: If you get stuck, don't forget about Walt Whitman's multitudes. Try asking yourself what your audience's pain points, or challenges, are as a Human Person, Role, and Brand. As a human person, consider their feelings, fears, ego, and daily life. As a role, consider their specific objectives. As a brand, consider how they need to 'show up' and be perceived.

YOUR TURN

Take no more than 15 minutes now to jot down, in bullet point format, the pain points you know your audience has relating to your products and services. Start by considering common questions they ask you and the frustrations or more profound problems that may lurk beneath them.

Also, consider whether that customer group might have content-specific pain points or challenges. Are they, for example, looking for more education or insight about what you offer? Or how products in your category might compare to one another? Might they need examples of what you do or provide or how you've helped others better understand how you can help them?

I've gathered a few more guiding questions to get you thinking:

- Relating to this customer group's jobs to be done, what challenges, obstacles, or blockers are they coming up against?

- Is there anything they don't know or can't do—that maybe you do or can—that could help them solve their problem?

- Where might they feel most frustrated or annoyed about their current situation or state?

- What might happen (what are the consequences) if your customers don't solve their problems? Consider cost and finances here, as well as emotional states.

- How are they solving this problem now? What solutions or workarounds do they use?

Gains

Determining what your audience seeks to gain from your content is your next challenge. Note that this is slightly different from figuring out what your audience seeks to gain from your products or services— although this will be similar.

Please note that the gain points for one audience segment or persona will often differ from those of another, so you'll want to do this exercise for each of your key segments.

What you want to do here, in a nutshell, is list the specific gains or benefits that your particular audience members might be seeking when they come across or search for your content—which might include your website, landing pages, specific campaigns, social media, video content, and more.

These top-of-mind benefits, or gains, are just a little different than the JTBDs, which involve digging beneath the surface a little to uncover the underlying task they're out to accomplish by "hiring" your content.

Here's an example from my own experience with a mobile fitness app for busy women:

The customer pain point (this one's a frustration)

A working mom is frustrated and demoralized by expensive fitness services whose marketing feature impossibly fits women with six-packs. Her feeds are overloaded with this kind of impossible imagery. She just wants to feel more fit and better about herself.

A related gain

From our product or service (in this case, a mobile fitness app), this working mom can gain convenience delivered in a realistic way (shorter workouts, different levels, etc.) and guidance from fantastic trainers. Not having to dress up to go to the gym is a bonus. Hoorah!

From our content? We can make her feel like she's found the right community. We can showcase the inspiration that the community provides and show her that there are others out there who feel like her—working moms who are just trying to squeeze in workouts when they can—getting healthy and fit when she's taking an IG break. Our content can make her feel seen. It can also educate her about what our app does, showing her those shorter workouts, different levels, fabulous trainers, etc.

> **HOT TIP:** To identify your customer content gains, respond to the customer content pains you just identified. Pains represent the problems, challenges, and issues customers want to avoid or eliminate, so ensure that your content value proposition effectively addresses those audiences' needs and desires.

And don't forget to prioritize. After you've brainstormed your gains, take a moment to prioritize them based on their importance to each audience segment. Some gains will be more valuable than others to your audiences—and by understanding which gains are most significant, you can focus your efforts on delivering the highest-value content to your most important audiences.

Forge & Spark Example

For our Lucy persona we have identified the following Gains:

- Thoughtful, premium-quality content impresses their audience and makes them look savvy & smart

- Clear business results and content aligned with brand purpose & values

- Their team is learning from us and is able to strategize/create content more effectively

- They love working with a thoroughly professional (and fun!) team that can be trusted

In this example, you'll note that each of our 'gain' points corresponds to a pain point, and prioritizes what our content and messaging (rather than services) can most effectively offer Lucy.

They have limited time, so we ensure that we develop lots of 'quick bite' content that's not just fluff. We always try to make it practical, and truly aimed at helping them solve one of her pressing challenges.

Lucy can't keep up, so we quick bits of education for social media as well as case studies that show how others addressed similar challenges, offering assistance and inspiration.

Lucy doubts her skills as a marketer, so we deliver easy-to-follow educational content such as tips, insights, templates, and tools to elevate their knowledge and capabilities, all while demonstrating that we've got the expertise to help and support, if needed.

They feel embarrassed by the quality of their content, so in our content we try to find realistic examples to inspire, illustrating what good could practically look like. In our newsletter, we often showcase brand content from small organizations that inspires us, including ideas and techniques used, with our take on why it's good and how to do it.

YOUR TURN

Take a moment now and review your list of audience pain points, then try to respond to each of them with a possible benefit or gain that your content could provide that is important to them. Consider:

- If they've got a pain point or challenge or a problem they're frustrated with, how might your content help them?
- Considering their JTBDs (those bigger-picture jobs they need to sort out), what might they need your content to do for them?

Other things to consider:

Could your content provide educational value? People look for, and appreciate, content that provides valuable information, insights, or knowledge, and that helps them learn something or stay on top of news or trends.

How might your content solve a problem for your audience? Does or could your content offer practical solutions to something that's bugging them? Audiences love and value how-to content, guides, and specific, actionable tips that they can follow to address an annoying problem or challenge..

Can you help your audience save time and effort? Good content well-presented has the potential to help your audience simplify their life or save time or effort, which can be a huge gain for busy people. You might break down complex information, provide tips or hacks, unique insight, time-saving tools, templates, or systems, or present tough-to-absorb content in manageable chunks.

Beyond practicality, could your content tell a good story ... and deliver the feels? People who tell stories that make people laugh or cry are popular at parties and in life, and there's a reason for that: as humans, we're hardwired to find narratives emotionally fulfilling. Stories have a unique power to spark emotional responses because they trigger the release of neurochemicals like dopamine, oxytocin, and endorphins. These are all chemicals tied to focus, empathy, and a sense of well-being. It's a natural reaction that makes stories captivating and deeply meaningful to each of us. Your audience might just love you for telling a good one.

If you're short on deep storytelling, might your content tickle, entertain, or delight? Short of rich brand storytelling, consider how your content might entertain, engage, or delight the people you want to do business with. Think fun, funny, or clever takes that captivates or offers a break from the humdrum.

Could you inspire, cheer on, or motivate your audience? Few things make me feel better than feeling like someone (yes, even a brand) gets me and has my back. We all need a little cheering-on from time to time. So consider sharing success stories, uplifting messages, or even an occasional nudge towards self-betterment (ideally without sounding holier-than).

Speaking of 'seen-ness,' could your content make your audience feel understood? Content that helps customers feel validated, understood, or part of a community—there's that sense of "attachment" that Gabor Maté speaks of—can be a significant gain point because it's a core need and simply feels good. As Maya Angelou observes, people tend to forget the specifics of what you say and do but will remember how you make them feel.

You can, and should, outline gain points that are unique to your brand and audiences. The simplest place to start is by reviewing the pain points you've identified, to consider how you might potentially use content to address, or alleviate them. And don't forget to review your persona's jobs, too. If there's a way for your content to help them complete a job, that's a major win.

And there you have it: your content's value proposition.

Ta-da! Look back over your work. What insights have you uncovered about your audience? Are you more clear about who your audience is, what they need to accomplish, the challenges they face, and the content you provide to make them feel seen, supported, and grateful to you or your brand?

You may have some distance to go in your messaging journey but give yourself props for starting the thinking and the work. You'll get there.

At this stage, we aim to see the world from our audience's viewpoint to figure out **what we need to express in our messaging to prompt action to meet our business goals.** And that's the heart of messaging.

"I've learned that people will forget what you said, people will forget what you did, but people will never forget how you made them feel."

~MAYA ANGELOU

CHAPTER 8

EFFECTIVE MESSAGING STATEMENTS

Your work on your OKRs, personas, and messaging framework will give you clarity and understanding about what you need to accomplish with your content, who you want to reach, and what they most want and need from your content. You are now ready, grasshopper, to craft your messaging statements.

Whether you consider yourself a writer or not, getting your messaging statements down on paper (or screen) FEELS hard—until you start. Isn't that true of so many things in life?

But what's most important to remember when you're setting out to craft authentic messaging for your brand is simply this: Get it out of your head! Turn 'vapour into paper,' as it were, without considering the quality of what you're documenting just yet. You might think of this next bit of work as—to use Ann Lamott's excellent phrase—a "shitty first draft."

Just get it down—even roughly—then fine-tune later. I give you full permission.

Your Most Important Messaging Statements

One of the first questions you'll want to ask yourself is, what kind of messaging do you most want and need? The answer will be different for different brands, industries, and people.

If you are only going to cover basic messaging, I suggest developing the following three important Messaging Statements:

- Core Brand Message

- Value Proposition Messaging

- Purpose & Values Messaging

Next, in order of priority, I'd suggest developing the following:

- Transformation Messaging

- Positioning Messaging

- Visual Messaging

Your Core Brand Message

Your Core Brand Message is the foundation of all your other messaging. It's a statement that captures what your brand stands for and sets you apart from your competition. It should be short, powerful, and memorable. Ideally, when finished, this message should be unique and relevant to the brand's identity and purpose. It should also be true wherever an audience encounters it, so it needs to be consistent across all marketing channels and touchpoints.

One straightforward way to begin thinking about this is by asking yourself how you want your brand to be perceived. It's essential to see your brand from an external perspective and consider who is unfamiliar with you, what you offer, or how you can benefit them.

Ask yourself this question now: How do you hope your most crucial audience sees or perceives your brand?

When we ask our clients this question, we receive responses like the following. They:

- Want to be perceived as a growing/successful/helpful company or service provider
- Hope to be seen as a brand that sustainably generates value for stakeholders
- Want to attract an audience they're not currently reaching or making traction with
- Would like to be recognized for X values/qualities (such as intelligence, thought leader)
- Want to be seen as helping people to X
- Wish they were known as a company that benefits X's audience and its employees, partners, communities, etc.
- Want to be known as a high performer / good community member, etc.

These statements alone can get you thinking about how you want to 'show up' in the world for a) what you offer, do, and/or are known for and b) why that matters to your audience. And this is the crux of the core brand message: It's that elusive intersection of what you bring to the table with how it benefits your audience.

This is the most critical question we use in our workshops to get at the core brand message:

> What key things do you want to communicate in your content that also results in some benefit (or pain relief) for your audience?

Break this challenge into two equal parts:

a) What your company or brand offers
b) Why it matters to your audience

An Example: The Forge & Spark Core Brand Message

Long Version: Forge & Spark is a women-led, certified B Corp content agency that partners with purpose-driven brands to craft premium-quality, impactful content. With our experienced and integrity-driven team, we empower clients to confidently share their stories, knowing their content will resonate and drive meaningful change.

Short & Sweet Version: Forge & Spark, a women-led B Corp, partners with purpose-driven brands to create impactful, high-quality content marketing that authentically shares their stories and drives meaningful change.

That's not bad, right? Ask me again in a year or two; it'll be subtly different. Remember to keep tweaking and evolving as your business does.

Hot AI Prompt

You don't have to do all this on your own. Try the following working prompt to figure out your core brand messaging.

Fill in these blanks first:

[Your Brand] is a [details about your company including how you classify yourself]. We [describe what you do or offer] with [describe the kinds of values or approach you use]. Our work benefits our audience because [details about your primary persona] gets/feels/earns [details about the gains your business provides].

Then try this prompt:

"If a core brand message is a statement encapsulating what you offer (that you most want to be known for) and why that matters to your audience, please draft a core brand message statement for [Your Brand]."

Value Proposition Messaging

A Value Proposition statement lives at the intersection between your **solution** to a specific customer's problem, the **advantage** you offer over your competitors, and the **benefits** that customers can expect. A killer value proposition statement shows your customers how you can help them tackle their challenges head-on and achieve the gains they want, all using your brand's tone of voice. Keep the final message short and straight to the point.

Note, too, that you can have more than one value proposition message, addressing the challenges and benefits you most want to highlight— perhaps for various customers. The key is to consider how to speak to one benefit or pain point at a time.

How to Efficiently Get to Your Value Proposition Message: One Pain or Gain at a Time

The good news here is that you will already have considered defining your audience's and customers' challenges and how they can most benefit from what you offer or provide. Thus, you'll want to refer back to your Messaging Spreadsheet, specifically those pains and gains columns you have already filled in for each of your target audience groups.

Start by choosing just one of those pain or gain points. For illustrative purposes, I'll start with one of our target audience's most cited pain points: that feeling of embarrassment, shame, and uncertainty that tells them they're probably not doing content right to accomplish their business goals.

Here, then, is where you'll ask yourself the following questions:

What's the solution you provide as a company or brand to alleviate this pain point?

F&S Answer: Premium-quality, beautiful, on-brand content to market our clients' business. Specifically, efficiently-produced, search-optimized long-form content promoted through social media, tailored to our clients' brands, and strategically delivered to meet their business goals.

What's the value of alleviating that pain point (if different than your solution?

F&S Answer: A feeling of relief and confidence that it's not only being executed beyond their standards – but that they don't even have to think about it anymore.

What's different about your solution from that of your competitors?

F&S Answer: Our deep experience in content marketing, our senior-level content marketing teams, and our commitment to quality and authenticity are among the reasons why experienced senior-level pros work thoughtfully and with care using a proven framework that goes well beyond what AI or junior writers from Upwork could ever offer.

What's the outcome or significant benefit you provide that matters to your audience?

F&S Answer: Targeted business results, ease of partnership with our warm and kind teams, commitment to their success,

Our Draft Value Proposition Statement for this pain point:

We translate your content overwhelm into confidence with premium, on-brand content that looks and sounds right and drives positive results. Our experienced, senior-level teams handle everything with care and focused attention so you can feel proud of your content and focus on what you do best.

As you'll see, I've tried to be a bit specific about what content marketing can be and about our specific solution (videos, blogs, and social posts in a thoughtfully organized content calendar), how we're different (our professional and premium-quality production), and the benefits to the audience (confidence, relief, and beautiful results).

Hot AI Prompt:

Value Proposition Messaging to Address Specific Pain Points

Complete this work first:

What's the solution you provide as a company or brand to alleviate this pain point? [Your solution]

What's the value of alleviating that pain point (if different than your solution)? [Describe the emotional or practical value of your work]

What's different about your solution from that of your competitors? [Describe what makes you different and better than others in your field]

Then try this prompt:

"If value proposition messaging is a short statement showcasing how you help your customers/clients to solve their problems, alleviate their key pain points, and/or tackle their challenges head-on, what is a value proposition messaging statement [Your Brand] can use to address a key client pain point of [identify one of your audience's key pain points]."

Incredible, yes? You'll want to edit and personalize the results, of course, so that they are accurate and feel right for your brand. This work is what will make a good value proposition statement great *for you.*

As you build out your messaging framework, capture each statement and your work in your spreadsheet or somewhere you and your team can actively and regularly access it.

You really can't overdo the value proposition statements. Not only will they help you think and write (or cut and paste!) when you need to create an ad, post, or web copy—or guide someone else in doing so—but you'll also really be thinking through the value to your customers of what you offer. The process is eye-opening even to seasoned writers and business owners.

Creating an Overarching Value Prop Statement for Your Brand

Going beyond specific pain point messaging, now, try the same approach with your overarching brand. The process is the same. Here's an example of the work we completed, followed by a suggested AI prompt you might use to complete your own.

The solution we provide: Premium-quality, beautiful, on-brand content to market our clients' business, strategically delivered to meet their business goals.

The core value we provide: Thoughtful on-brand content brands can truly take pride in because it authentically expresses who they are as a values-led business.

A differentiator that helps us stand out from competitors: Our deep experience in content marketing, our senior-level content marketing teams, and our commitment to quality and authenticity.

Outcomes to highlight: Targeted business results, ease of partnership with our warm and kind teams, commitment to their success, a feeling of relief and confidence that content marketing is not only being executed beyond their standards but that they don't even have to think about it anymore.

Our Value Proposition Messaging Statement

We craft beautiful, on-brand content that purpose-driven businesses can truly be proud of. Our experienced teams express your brand with care and experience, delivering strategic results while making your marketing feel effortless and authentically you.

Now you give it a go ...

Hot AI Prompt:

Value Proposition Messaging for Your Brand

Do this work:

- The solution we provide is: [provide details about the products or services you offer]

- The core value we provide is: [provide details about the value you offer]

- A differentiator that helps us stand out from our competitors is: [provide details about your differentiating factors]

- Outcomes we want to highlight in our Value Proposition Messaging Statement include: [provide details about what makes you different from your competitors].

Then try this prompt:

"If a Value Proposition Messaging Statement is a short statement showcasing how you help your customers/clients to solve their problems, alleviate their key pain points, and/or tackle their challenges head-on, please develop a Value Proposition Statement for [Your Brand] based on the following information: [Enter your previous work here in entirety]."

More Examples of Solid Brand Value Proposition Messaging

Mailchimp

We found this statement on one of Mailchimp's landing pages, and it qualifies as a great value proposition statement.

TURN EMAILS INTO REVENUE

Win new customers with the #1 email marketing and automations brand that recommends ways to get more opens, clicks, and sales

It's got it all, truly. The solution they provide is clear within the statement: It's all about email marketing and automation. They weave in the value and benefit of this solution right at the top ("Turn Emails into Revenue") and then again at the bottom, identifying benefits and outcomes ("more opens, clicks, and sales"). The supporting statement also explains how it's different and better than other solutions ("the #1 email marketing and automations brand"). It's efficient and effective, too.

Here are a few other examples we've come across:

Patagonia:	"We're in business to save our home planet. We aim to use the resources we have—our business, our investments, our voice, and our imaginations—to do something about it."
Hootsuite:	"Hootsuite is the global leader in social media management, trusted by more than 18 million customers and employees at 80% of the Fortune 1000."
Warby Parker:	"Warby Parker was founded with a rebellious spirit and a lofty objective: to offer designer eyewear at a revolutionary price, while leading the way for socially conscious businesses."
Tentree:	"We're planting 1 billion trees by 2030 to drastically reduce climate change and revitalize ecosystems around the world. We plant 10 trees for every item purchased in our store."
Ben & Jerry's:	"We make the best possible ice cream in the best possible way. We source Non-GMO ingredients, Fairtrade, and cage-free eggs. Our ice cream is made with milk & cream from happy cows."
Danone:	"Danone's mission is to bring health through food to as many people as possible. The company aims to inspire healthier and more sustainable eating and drinking practices."

Seventh Generation:	"We're on a mission to transform the world into a healthy, sustainable & equitable place for the next seven generations."
New Belgium Brewing:	"We manifest our love and talent by crafting our customers' favourite brands and proving business can be a force for good."
Kickstarter:	"Our mission is to help bring creative projects to life. We believe that art and creative expression are essential to a healthy and vibrant society."

These value propositions clearly communicate how each brand solves customer problems or addresses key pain points while also showcasing their commitment to purpose and positive impact. This kind of messaging underpins much of each brand's marketing.

Purpose & Values Messaging

Purpose messaging is, in a nutshell, messaging that communicates your brand or organisational purpose so that you can speak confidently and eloquently about your 'why.' This kind of messaging may not always show up overtly in your marketing but should underline 'how you show up' in your content marketing.

For purpose-led brands, crafting the right statements to capture and illustrate your purpose and values can have several advantages.

For business owners like me, these statements are incredibly powerful. I use them all the time—on proposals, grant applications, in company descriptions, and in short versions of my own bio. So, it's a valuable exercise to work out a good long-form and short-form version of your own purpose statement.

Again, the win here is that you've already worked on yours, way back in Chapter 2. Let's circle back to your chart and pull up what you drafted.

Then let's work on it in your framework and make it useful for your everyday use.

I'm going to recommend drafting your statement in a few ways that are customised for you.

Here are the ones I most commonly use.

- **The paragraph/working version**: This can be long and imperfect. Use it to capture all your thoughts and then tweak it for use as a short paragraph you can easily use in presentations, website copy, sales decks, award applications, or other marketing materials.

- **The short and sweet version**: Think of this as your elevator pitch. Keep it memorable so that everyone on your team learns it by heart.

Example of Our Purpose Messaging Statement

Here is the purpose statement we actively use at Forge & Spark, as noted previously:

To foster genuine connection, even in marketing. We bring authenticity and power to premium-quality marketing content, helping companies with purpose to flourish.

The short & sweet version:

Authentic content for positive impact

Hot AI Prompt:

Crafting Your Purpose & Values Statement

We didn't rely on AI to draft our purpose statement, but we gained value by performing this quick, revealing exercise.

Then try this prompt:

"If a purpose & values messaging statement is a short statement that captures the passion and purpose behind what you do as a business, and should contribute to your positioning, messaging, and storytelling, please draft a purpose & values messaging statement for Forge & Spark based on the following information: [Cut and paste or write out all you know about your company purpose, values, and content marketing mission, as worked out in Chapters 3 and 4.]"

Here's what I got when I performed this exercise, pasting in Forge & Spark's Purpose Statement, Mission Statement, and detailed Company Values from our Employee Handbook:

At Forge & Spark, we're passionate about fostering genuine connections through authentic, high-quality content. We partner with purpose-led businesses to amplify their impact, believing that true societal change begins with honest communication. Guided by our values of creative excellence, firm kindness, resourceful entrepreneurialism, collaborative strength, and integrity, we strive to be the trusted agency for those committed to making a positive difference in the world.

And a short and sweet version? My Chat GPT Shanbot suggested this:

Forge & Spark creates authentic, high-quality content to help purpose-led businesses drive meaningful change.

Not bad. You might see this messaging show up in our content in the future!

Other Kinds of Messages You Might Want to Create

Transformation Messaging

How are you going to change your audience's lives with your brand, product, or service—or with the content you create? This kind of messaging is a little like creating a picture of what your customer's world will be like.

I actually hadn't crafted a transformation messaging statement for Forge & Spark, so I just asked Perplexity AI to research our mission, services, and target audience to understand how we transform our customers' lives and to craft a transformation messaging statement based on our website content.

Here's what I got back:

When you partner with Forge & Spark Media, you're not just getting a content agency—you're gaining a strategic ally in your mission to create positive change. Our authentic, intelligent content and social media marketing services help purpose-driven businesses like yours share your story, reach your target audience, and inspire meaningful action. By working with us, you'll be able to grow your impact while staying true to your values, ultimately creating a better world for your customers, your community, and the planet.

Guess what? With just a few tweaks, I added that to our website.

Grow Your Business With Better Content.

Effective content marketing captivates, builds trust, and drives meaningful action. But creating exceptional content can be overwhelming without the right support—and that's where we come in.

As a passionate, women-led team, we're more than just your content partner; we're your strategic ally in your mission to create positive change. With smart content marketing strategy and warm, efficient support, we help purpose-driven businesses like yours share your story, engage your audience, and inspire action. Together, we'll elevate your impact and ensure your values shine through every piece of content.

A few great examples of transformation messaging sources through Perplexity:

Fairware: Fairware helps you create meaningful branded merchandise that aligns with your values. Our ethically-sourced, eco-friendly products allow you to showcase your brand while supporting fair labour practices and reducing environmental impact.

Bullfrog Power: By choosing Bullfrog Power, you're not just powering your home or business—you're supporting the growth of renewable energy in Canada. Our green energy solutions help you reduce your environmental impact and contribute to a cleaner, healthier future.

Greyston Bakery: When you enjoy a Greyston Bakery brownie, you're not just indulging in a delicious treat—you're supporting our open hiring model, which provides job opportunities to individuals who have faced barriers to employment.

Dr. Bronner's: When you use Dr. Bronner's soaps, you're not just cleaning your body—you're supporting our mission to create a more just and sustainable world. We invest in fair trade, organic agriculture, and social justice initiatives to make a positive impact.

Ella's Kitchen: Ella's Kitchen helps you nourish your baby with organic, nutritious food while supporting our commitment to sustainability and social responsibility. By choosing our products, you're investing in your child's health and the health of the planet.

Beau's All Natural Brewing: When you drink Beau's beer, you're not just enjoying a delicious craft brew—you're supporting our commitment to organic ingredients, sustainable practices, and community involvement. We donate a portion of our profits to local charities and environmental initiatives.

Allbirds: When you wear Allbirds shoes, you're not just investing in your comfort—you're supporting our commitment to sustainability. Our shoes are made from renewable materials, reducing your carbon footprint with every step.

Looking at the Allbirds messaging, we can see it show up in an Allbirds press release[19] announcing leadership promotions, demonstrating how brands can weave this kind of messaging into official communications, content, and overarching brand narrative.

"Headquartered in San Francisco, Allbirds is a global lifestyle brand that innovates with naturally derived materials to make better footwear and apparel products in a better way, while treading lighter on the planet. Allbirds's story began with superfine New Zealand merino wool and has since evolved to include a eucalyptus tree fibre knit fabric and a sugarcane-based EVA SweetFoam®, castor bean oil-based SwiftFoam™, and Plant Leather."

The press release emphasizes Allbirds' use of sustainable, naturally derived materials in their products, directly tying back to the transformation messaging statement about reducing the customer's carbon footprint by wearing Allbirds shoes made from renewable materials.

Positioning Messaging

Crafting your brand's positioning is an art in itself, and I don't presume to be an expert. Read the marvellous April Dunford for that. But I've helped many companies with their positioning statements—which really boil down to explaining what you offer in the context of a particular market need. The four main elements of a positioning statement generally include:

- The target audience you serve

- Your marketing category (where you're competing)

- How you're different than your competitors

- Benefits to your audience and/or pains you address

And for purpose- or values-led businesses, I would also recommend touching on your brand purpose, identity, and values in your positioning statements since these are, indeed, some of the things that likely make you stand apart.

Think of the positioning statement, then, as an extension of your overall value proposition, with a bit more emphasis on describing who your target customer is and <u>why</u> you do what you do.

Some Good Examples:

"We're Wistia. We make marketing software, video series, and educational content based on the belief that anyone can use video to grow their business and their brand."

This statement highlights the brand's core belief that "anyone can use video to grow their business and brand." Interestingly they don't really describe their products—which are varied—rather choosing to focus on their intention, which is a solid positioning strategy.

Apple revolutionized personal technology with the introduction of the Macintosh in 1984. Today, Apple leads the world in innovation with [the] iPhone, iPad, Mac, Apple Watch, and Apple TV. Apple's five software platforms—iOS, iPadOS, macOS, watchOS, and tvOS—provide seamless experiences across all Apple devices and empower people with breakthrough services, including the App Store, Apple Music, Apple Pay, and iCloud. Apple's more than 100,000 employees are dedicated to making the best products on earth, and to leaving the world better than we found it.

Sources:

Apple's Investor Relations website:
https://investor.apple.com/corporate-governance/governance-documents/default.aspx

Panmore Institute:
https://panmore.com/apple-mission-statement-vision-statement

Business Strategy Hub:
https://bstrategyhub.com/apple-mission-statement-vision-core-values/

How's that for comprehensive? They often include this positioning statement near the end of their press releases to reinforce their history and credibility and to underscore the breadth of their platforms and offerings. It's also featured on their website (specifically the "Apple Leadership" page under the "About Apple" section).

Competition Messaging: Consider How to Position Against Your Competition, Too

Competition Messaging is a clear, concise way to communicate how your brand stands out in your particular market. It includes or summarizes your unique value proposition and highlights the competitive advantages that make your brand distinct from your rivals. I consider this underlying messaging (and a part of positioning) that you want to get across to set your brand apart from the rest rather than a formal statement.

Here are a few examples of companies that nail this. I've summarized their overall messaging again, as most don't have formal statements.

Slack: Slack is where the right people, information, and tools come together to get work done seamlessly. Whether you're a Fortune 100 company or a small business, millions worldwide trust Slack to connect their teams and streamline their operations. Unlike competitors, Slack fosters genuine social interaction and healthy competition within teams, making collaboration as dynamic as it is effective.

Apple: For those who demand the best in personal computing and mobile devices, Apple is the leader in innovation. Unlike others, Apple doesn't just push boundaries in technology; it also prioritizes the impact its products and processes have on both customers and the planet. This forward-thinking approach is evident in everything from their web copy to their advertising.

Warby Parker: Warby Parker was built on a rebellious spirit and a bold goal: offering designer eyewear at a price that disrupts the industry while championing social responsibility. Unlike traditional retailers,

Warby Parker designs in-house and sells directly to you, cutting out the middleman and passing the savings on to you.

Dollar Shave Club: For guys who refuse to overpay for a great shave, Dollar Shave Club delivers high-quality razors straight to your door at a fraction of the cost. No gimmicks, no vibrating handles, no flashy ads— just top-notch blades for a few bucks a month.

Tesla: For those who care about the environment and high performance, Tesla offers the most advanced and stylish electric vehicles out there. Unlike traditional automakers, Tesla is laser-focused on making affordable electric cars to accelerate the world's shift to sustainable energy.

Note that these examples highlight each brand's unique selling proposition and how they stand out from their competitors. By emphasizing their differentiators—whether innovation, affordability, convenience, or social responsibility—these brands show how they want to be seen as better and more valuable to target customers than other players in their field.

Forge & Spark Example

As for us? Our underlying Competitive Messaging focuses on a few key points to stand apart:

- Specialization in working with purpose-driven brands (many agencies focus on specific verticals rather than values)

- B Corp certification and commitment to using business for good (a lot of agencies don't have this accreditation)

- Senior-level, experienced content pros who lead monthly strategy and create or oversee every content deliverable (many agencies assign juniors to execute on content, while senior leaders are there in name only)

We try to weave these points into our content and messaging on various channels, aiming to set ourselves apart from other agencies and consultants as a values-oriented, purpose-driven content agency that's a true partner, deeply invested in our clients' success and impact.

Visual Messaging

Visual messaging is near and dear to our hearts at Forge & Spark. It's an absolutely critical element in the success of any brand's content marketing. The reason I place it a little lower in my list of critical messaging is that it's extremely difficult to get right until you nail your other messaging.

Visual messaging refers to the strategic use of visual elements like logos, colours, fonts, images, videos, and graphics to communicate your brand's identity, values, and purpose. It goes well beyond words to help brands convey information, build emotional connections with their audience, and create a distinct, recognizable identity that sets them apart from competitors.

At Forge & Spark, our process of developing visual content is rooted in messaging. Lara Kroeker, our Creative Director, is fond of pointing out that "content leads design." Designers, in other words, need to have clarity about what needs to be expressed before they can properly express it visually. Your messaging framework will provide precisely this clarity to your designers.

Our process to develop content marketing for clients is to complete clear OKRs, develop empathetic personas, and create messaging maps for each persona that identify their jobs, pains, and gains before creating visual design systems for the brand to explore visual ways to bring who you are and what you want to say as a brand to life.

How might you begin?

I'd suggest beginning with a visual audit of your brand visuals, including logos, websites, ads, social media, marketing collateral, etc. You'll want to organize these assets to identify patterns and inconsistencies and assess challenges and opportunities to create a cohesive visual system. Of course, pull in your non-visual brand components like brand voice, personality, and positioning to inform future visual design.

Next, it's all about aligning your visuals with your brand identity and, most importantly, messaging. Your visual messaging should authentically represent your brand's unique identity, values, and purpose.

Messaging and content drive design, so defining your brand personality, voice, and positioning (all the good stuff you're doing right now) will be vital in developing visuals that reinforce the right message. For example, a friendly, optimistic brand voice might translate to brighter colours and lighter fonts, while an authoritative one suggests deeper hues and classic typefaces.

In your brand's visual messaging, you'll want to:

- **Ensure consistency:** Cohesive visuals across all brand touchpoints are crucial to building trust and recognition. Forge & Spark emphasizes the importance of creating practical tools like style guides and asset libraries to ensure brand elements are being used consistently, both internally and externally.

- **Stand out from the pack:** Strong visual messaging and an effective visual identity should set your brand apart in the market. We recommend analysing competitors' visual styles to identify opportunities to differentiate, even when using common elements like stock photos. Finding a distinctive visual voice is key.

- **Optimize for your unique audience:** Ultimately, your visual messaging should be tailored to resonate with your specific target audience. You can, for example, choose colours, fonts, imagery, and graphics that will appeal to and engage your ideal customers.

In the end, visual messaging uses the same strategic, audience-centric approach as your overall brand messaging. So, once you've got your messaging clear, take a shot at refreshing your visual brand and see what visual impact emerges. We did this with our latest brand refresh and emerged with a fresh look and feel that genuinely surprised and delighted me. "It just feels more like us" is ultimately what you're going for.

Voice & Tone Messaging

Communication is at the heart of every relationship. It's how we connect, build trust, and understand one another. And it's not just about words—it's about how those words are delivered, interpreted, and felt. Communication is an inherently creative act; it's the expression of feeling, insight, and perception. It's what makes us human.

For brands, the challenge is that so much of communication goes beyond the words themselves. The underlying tone, intent, and personality in your messaging play a vital role in how your audience interprets and feels about what you say. This is why defining your brand voice and tone is crucial. It shapes not just the content you share, but how people experience and connect with your brand on a deeper, more emotional level.

Whenever we start working with a new client, one of our first questions is about their brand voice. If they haven't defined it as part of their brand guidelines, we make that step one—because without a consistent and well-thought-out voice, even the best messaging can fall flat or feel disconnected.

When defining your brand voice, it's important to understand not only how you want to sound but also what to avoid. Here are some key voice characteristics, along with examples of how they might come across in your messaging—and how they shouldn't:

1. Authoritative

- *What This Means for Your Brand*: Share your expert knowledge with confidence, positioning yourself as a trusted guide.

- *But It's NOT*: Talking down to your audience or making them feel uninformed.

- *Write Like This*: "Here's what we recommend based on our years of experience..."

- *Don't Write Like This*: "We know better than you, so just follow this."

2. Conversational

- *What This Means for Your Brand*: Engage your audience with warmth and openness, making them feel like you're having a real conversation.

- *But It's NOT*: Sloppy, overly casual, or unprofessional.

- *Write Like This*: "Let's talk about what this means for you..."

- *Don't Write Like This*: "Hey, what's up, folks!"

3. Funny

- *What This Means for Your Brand*: Use humour to create connection, but keep it within boundaries that suit your brand and audience.

- *But It's NOT*: Offensive, crass, or inappropriate.

- *Write Like This*: "We know Mondays can be tough, here's how we can help."

- *Don't Write Like This*: "Guess you hate Mondays, too. Suck it up!

Tone: Varying Your Approach

While your brand voice should stay consistent, your tone can and should shift depending on the context or platform. What works for a social post on Instagram may not resonate in an email to stakeholders or in a detailed whitepaper. The key is to keep your tone aligned with your core voice.

Be mindful of the audience's expectations on each channel. It's tempting to try something playful or edgy on social media, but be sure it fits the situation. Searching for "tone-deaf marketing" will reveal countless examples of brands that missed the mark by trying to sound trendy or provocative without truly understanding their audience.

Capturing Voice and Tone in Your Framework

To ensure consistency across your marketing, document your brand voice and tone guidelines within your messaging framework. Include clear examples of what your voice sounds like and how your tone might vary. This document will be essential for anyone creating content for your brand, from social media managers to copywriters.

By doing this work upfront, you'll not only create more cohesive messaging but also ensure your content connects more authentically with your audience.

Customizing Your Messaging for Unique Scenarios

There's no end to the kinds of messages you can create based on that magical intersection of what you need to communicate with what your audience most needs from you. Other kinds of messaging, for example, might include:

- Messaging about your specific products or services

- Conversion messaging to ensure that you (and your audiences) accomplish a particular objective

- Narrative messaging that tells a mini-story about an aspect of your business

- Thought leadership messaging to establish your authority and credibility

- Educational messaging to teach your audience something about your product, services, or area of expertise

- Emotional messaging to create genuine connection and to inspire a specific feeling

- Specific values messaging to highlight a particular core value and your commitment to that value

- Community-building messaging to cultivate a true sense of belonging and community within your audience

- Crisis messaging to protect your brand reputation, addressing and/or mitigating negative publicity, crises, or controversies to protect the brand's reputation.

In the next chapter, we'll look at ways to identify the priority areas you'll need messaging for and develop actionable 'recipes' for putting your messaging to work.

CHAPTER 9

APPLYING YOUR MESSAGING

At this point in your messaging journey, I hope you're gaining clarity about the kinds of messaging that will serve you best. And if you've completed the messaging activities, you should have some pretty darned robust messaging to work with, providing you with a clear direction and focus.

But exactly how to use it in your day-to-day communications and content may be more of a mystery. In this chapter, we'll take a look at some ways to activate your messaging, empowering you to guide your internal and external communications and teams with confidence.

Broad Uses for Your Messaging Framework

Having a messaging framework in place does a couple of things brilliantly. First, it helps you and all those creating it—usually business owners and their senior-level teams and communication specialists—to get crystal clear on who you are as a business and brand, including having a clear and shared knowledge of how you can best serve and speak with your most important audiences, what makes you different and better than your competitors, and how your purpose informs what you do, and talk about as a brand. Not bad, right?

Secondarily, it serves as a documented reference point for others in your business to understand all of the above.

Your sales team, for example, can use your messaging framework to quickly understand the key differentiators you want to highlight, the benefits and pain points you want them to reference in their sales communications and meetings, and the underlying motivations or 'jobs' that drive your audiences and customers to learn more about you.

Any folks assisting with your business communications or PR can use your framework to efficiently digest the 'bullet point' messages they might choose from in their press releases and communicate with any of your partners or influencers you work with. They can also better understand your differentiators and how you are different from the companies offering similar products or services.

And finally, the key here for us as a content agency is using your messaging framework to help you, your teams, and any outside agencies or freelancers to quickly and effectively create the inbound content marketing—and external marketing, too—that's going to attract, engage, and endear your audience. Content like blogs, podcasts, video scripts, and more. This efficient approach will ensure your content is created quickly and resonates with your audience based on everything you know about them. Below I'll outline exactly how to apply your Messaging Framework to an effective content plan for your business.

In general, your messaging framework will help you to:

- Achieve a shared understanding within your company of what you do and why it matters

- Establish stories and narratives that everyone in the company understands and knows

- Create consistency in the way your teams talk about your work and products internally and externally

- Minimize any confused messaging to your audiences, maintaining consistent wording and prioritized messaging

- Guide your content marketing and content development efforts

So, to put your new messaging framework to good use, I'd heartily recommend that you review it, fill in what you can, and invite input from your key stakeholders. Once there, let's move on to action. Ready? Let's do it.

Make Your Messaging Actionable With Messaging Recipes

Need to talk about something specific but also keep it on-brand? Enter Messaging Recipes.

Messaging recipes are briefs that your organization can use to achieve specific results. They combine elements from your core messaging with specific marketing or sales information to create a full picture of what you want to say and how you want to show up to accomplish specific results in sales and marketing materials. And they should be easy to use and re-use; once you've gotten a recipe right, developing your messaging is a matter of getting stakeholders to simply answer a set of questions.

Creating your unique messaging recipes is easier than it may first appear. You've already developed your core messaging. This next bit can be as simple as adjusting and combining messages from your framework for specific use cases.

My trick is creating simple sheets within our Messaging Framework, adapting when and as needed. The beauty of the recipe approach to specific messaging is that armed with the guiding messaging framework you've created, you (or those who work with you) will be able to draft messaging recipes quickly and easily. It comes down to simply answering a series of questions.

Below, I've outlined my own set of rules for creating good messaging recipes:

1. Make them actionable.

No, you don't have to use spreadsheets. We use them because they're easy to cut and paste from and to classify different kinds of information without scrolling through a long document. But it's your choice. Put it in a Google Doc, in Miro or Figma, on a whiteboard—the format is all yours, as long as those doing your sales and marketing can easily and willingly find and use them.

2. Write short <u>and</u> extended versions of the copy you need.

I find it enormously helpful to include super short notes on the messaging concepts as well as more extended versions of copy that anyone on your team can cut and paste from for use or adaptation in documents, articles, or copy.

3. Customize for use.

Below, you'll find some sample recipes to use as a starting point. But by all means, cut out what's extraneous and add what's missing. Get creative and add, edit, remove, or even create your recipes from scratch. Your messaging must be unique to you.

And the more recipes you develop, the more skill you and your team will develop in the kitchen. Master Chef-dom is yours.

Product/Service Sample Messaging Recipe

Beyond describing your brand at a high level, you'll likely have cause to describe and sell products or services. If so, try this Product/Service Recipe.

It will give you and your team a quick overview of what's being discussed, who needs it, your audience's relationship with the pain points or benefits associated with the product/service, what the key value of the product/service is to your audience, and any particular features you'd like to highlight.

To use this recipe, you or stakeholders simply have to fill in the blanks in the right column, answering the questions provided. Keep it brief.

Messaging Recipe: Product/Service/Campaign	
The product/ service (or 'family')	What product or service are you discussing? Get specific about what this messaging applies to. It's sometimes easiest to start with a particular product, but you can also use this recipe to talk about a family or whole category of products/services.
The target audience	Consider which persona, audience segment, or kind of person this particular messaging recipe should address.
Audience pain points or challenges	What challenges, frustrations, or pain points do your target audience have in relation to this product/service? Choose 1-3 to focus on in your messaging.
Benefits from product/service	Perhaps found in the answer in the row above, what advantages or benefits does this product/service offer? Choose 1-3 to focus on in your messaging.
Product value proposition*	Very briefly describe the unique benefits and value that this product/service offers to your target audience.
Positioning	Building from the row above, how do you want this product/service to be perceived by your target audience in relation to your competitors? This might be about what your brand stands for, its unique benefits, and why people should choose it vs. alternatives.
Product features to highlight	What are the features of your product or service that will support or underline the value prop and positioning you identified above? No more than 5.
Terms and keywords for content creation	When you talk about this product, what key terms do you want to use? Pay close attention to keyword research and how your target audience searches for solutions to their challenges and pain points.
Long-form blurbs for cut-and-paste	This is space for gathering the copy you create around this product or service. Include links or whole paragraphs of text as you'd like.

*With this recipe, the trick is really in getting to the value proposition statement for that specific product or service. Here are my guesses as to what the product value proposition is for a few well-known products or services.

- **Spotify:** Unlimited access to millions of songs and podcasts anytime, anywhere. You're empowered to soundtrack your life based on your tastes and moods.

- **Numi Organic Tea:** You can savour every delicious sip knowing you're supporting ethical sourcing and environmental stewardship.

- **Apple AirPods Pro:** Redefine wireless audio / deliver a magical listening experience, seamlessly connecting to all your Apple devices.

- **Ecover Eco-Friendly Dish Soap:** Wash away grease and grime with the knowledge that you're minimizing your ecological footprint.

- **Seventh Generation Plant-Based Laundry Detergent**: Powerful cleaning and environmental responsibility.

An Example: Forge & Spark's Product/Service Recipe for Brand Content Kits	
The product/ service (or 'family')	Brand Content Kit (occasionally called Brand Kit) A design service that equips you with a visual design system along with branded content assets. You get 1:1 expert guidance to create a cohesive visual identity for your brand, all within the span of a week. It's a fast, personalized design service that delivers fresh branding and high-quality, ready-to-use visual content for solopreneurs and small businesses.
Your target audience	Junior Lucy: A purpose-driven solopreneur or small business owner with a vision for growth. They have high standards for their brand but are short on time and design resources. They need professional, agency-quality visuals that match their ambition without the overwhelming effort or the need for an in-house design team.

An Example: Forge & Spark's Product/Service Recipe for Brand Content Kits	
Audience pain points or challenges	• Inconsistent branding and visual quality across channels • Feeling like they're always starting from scratch with content and visuals • Frustration with "bad-looking" or "embarrassing" content • Lack of organization and systems in managing visual assets, leading to inefficiency and chaos
Benefits your audience gets from the product	• Access to a library of custom brand assets and templates designed by a professional Creative Director • An elevated, cohesive visual identity that reflects the true quality of their brand • A professional, polished look for all branded content, ensuring consistency across channels • The ability to easily bring their brand vision to life without needing to worry about a lack of in-house design expertise • Organized, ready-to-use content in a streamlined system that saves time and effort
Product value proposition	**In as little as a week**, we deliver a tailored **visual identity system** and a suite of branded content that's ready for use—allowing you to elevate your brand, maintain consistency, and save time with professional, custom-designed assets.
Your messaging positioning	As a small, purpose-driven agency, we understand what it's like to juggle many roles with limited resources. That's why we've designed the Brand Content Kit: to help you show up with confidence, consistency, and authenticity. Our thoughtful approach and deep respect for your vision and busy schedule allow us to deliver high-impact, professional visuals that align perfectly with your brand's needs.

An Example: Forge & Spark's Product/Service Recipe for Brand Content Kits	
The product features you want to highlight	• Efficient Delivery: A complete visual identity system delivered in just one week • 1:1 Guidance: Led by a professional Creative Director who works directly with you throughout the process • Designed for Practical Use: The kit includes everything from your core brand elements (logos, colour palettes, typography) to everyday content assets (social media templates, imagery), all organized in Canva for easy access and use
Terms and keywords for content creation	• Refer to the service as the Brand Content Kit. • Emphasize that the kit includes foundational brand assets and ready-to-use content. • Highlight the creation of a Visual Identity System, gathering all key elements (logo, palette, typography, imagery) into a Canva-based kit. • SEO Keywords: Content Creator Kit, Visual Content, Visual Content Marketing, Brand Content Kit, social media template
Long-form blurbs for cut-and-paste	The Brand Content Kit is a design service tailored for solopreneurs and small business owners who value high standards but lack the time and resources for in-house design work. In just one week, our professional design team, led by an experienced Creative Director, creates a complete visual identity system and a suite of branded content that's ready to use. From social media templates to logo design, the kit provides everything you need to present your brand with consistency and impact across all channels. We deliver all assets in a handy Canva kit, making it simple to maintain visual consistency and elevate your brand solo or with a team. With Forge & Spark's thoughtful, efficient approach, you'll save time, reduce the hassle of content creation, and achieve a polished, professional look that brings your brand vision to life.

An Example: Forge & Spark's Product/Service Recipe for Brand Content Kits	
Short and sweet version	The Brand Content Kit is a design service that provides a complete visual identity system and branded content, ensuring that your business has consistent, professional branding and ready-to-use materials across all channels—all delivered in as little as a week.

You can see the messaging at work in the sales page for our Brand Content Kits:

Get Authenticity, Consistency, And Impact

As a purpose-driven solopreneur or small business, you have a clear vision. But does your visual presence reflect that vision?

If you're struggling with **inconsistent branding, poor or inconsistent visual content**, or the **constant dread** of creating content from scratch, you might need the Brand Content Kit.

It's a done-for-you design service that equips you with a visual design system along with branded content assets.

You get 1:1 expert guidance to create not just a cohesive visual identity for your brand, but also high-quality, ready-to-use visual content, all in as little as a week.

Messaging Recipe for Thought Leadership and Trust

Another messaging recipe you may wish to document and practice is one to highlight your own expertise and impact—whether as an individual or a thought-leading brand. Here's our base recipe, which we customize for individual clients (and ourselves). I'll also share my own thought leadership recipe.

Note that this recipe focuses on just one primary OKR and persona. This is designed to keep the messaging simple and targeted. If you have additional objectives or audiences, simply complete the recipe for each.

Messaging Recipe for Thought Leadership and Trust	
Primary OKR	List at least one objective followed by a result you seek, based on developing your thought leadership content.
Target Audience	Consider which one persona, audience segment, or kind of person this particular messaging recipe should address.
Core Subject Matter	To accomplish your Primary OKR and engage the persona above to take notice, describe broadly what you're going to talk about. List up to 5 subject areas.
How You're Different	Consider how other people talk about the subject above, and describe how you can approach them uniquely.
Your Key Themes	Draft 3 themes: things you want to express in your content and/or that you want your audience to understand about you. These can be opinions, beliefs, hot takes, or things you find yourself always saying.
The Impact You're Seeking	The purpose of all this thought leadership ... what are you aiming to do here when sharing your expertise?
Call to Action	Don't forget to identify what you want your audience to do as a result of your content!

Our Example: My Thought Leadership Messaging Recipe	
Your OKRs	To establish myself as a purpose-led leader supporting other purpose-led leaders in achieving greater impact through content marketing Key results: Thought-provoking conversations on LinkedIn that grow my network and build trust, the right kinds of leads for the business
Target Audience	Purpose-led biz leaders and marketers concerned with communicating with greater power and integrity
Core Subject Matter	• Content Marketing for Thought Leadership & Trust Building • B Corp leadership / my and FS' journey • Authenticity in messaging • Clarity on goal setting / OKRs • Content Marketing and AI
How I'm Different	• I care a lot about authenticity. • My focus is on helping those who want to make a positive impact. • I was trained as a journalist and writer and care deeply about both saying what's true and saying it effectively for impact.
My Key Themes	• To be competitive, I believe companies need to develop content and marketing that showcases their unique value. • It's a noisy world with a lot of posturing and fakery. Other people believe that to sell things and grow a business, marketing has to be phony, that you have to be duplicitous, sneaky, and abandon your values. You don't. • There's too much crap content and messaging out there. If you're doing good work, there's a way to talk about it that can both feel good and be effective.
The Impact I'm Seeking	• Positive impact through business • Developing confidence and empowered expression among those whose voices in business often don't get heard • Elevating the quality and thoughtfulness of marketing content and business communication
Call to Action	Get in touch by email—let's chat!

Messaging Recipe for An Effective HomePage

Your website's homepage is often your first chance to make an impression on your audience, so it should effectively communicate your purpose, connect with your audience, and perhaps even move them to action (even if it's just to read on). You can make the most of this crucial touchpoint by crafting messaging that reflects your brand stories, values, and the specific needs of your target audiences. Using a blend of methodologies for telling an effective story on your home page, here's one way to structure and refine your homepage messaging to ensure it resonates deeply and effectively. This is a recipe I've used often with our clients, mixing and matching the order and priority of each section.

Messaging Recipe for An Effective HomePage	
Hero Section	The hero section is the first thing visitors see, so it should articulate your core brand promise clearly and concisely.
	Headline: Highlight the transformational value your brand delivers.
	Example: "Transforming Purpose into Impactful Action."
	Subheadline: Reinforce the emotional and practical benefits of your work.
	Example: "We help mission-driven leaders design strategies that inspire, connect, and create lasting change."
	Call-to-Action (CTA): Make it easy for visitors to take the next step.
	Example: "Start Your Journey" or "Book a Call/Consultation").
Pain Point / Problem Section	Your homepage should empathize with the challenges your audience faces and establish how your brand solves them.
	Example: "Your mission deserves to reach the people who need it most. Yet, without clear messaging or impactful content, even the best ideas can get lost. That's where we come in."
	This positions your brand as the trusted guide for overcoming obstacles while aligning with the audience's goals.

Messaging Recipe for An Effective HomePage	
Value / Gain Section	On your homepage you should also make it clear what benefit or gain your audience gets from working with you. Structure this section with visuals and concise messaging: Example: "We create authentic, human-centered solutions that help mission-driven leaders maximize their impact—without compromising their values."
Process / Approach Section	Somewhere on your homepage, make it clear to your audience what it's like to work with you (and ideally how simple and actionable it is). Use this section to make your audience feel supported and confident in your expertise. Breaking down your process into clear, approachable steps is one option to help build trust and reduce friction. Three-Step Process Example: • Understand Your Mission: Collaborate with you to clarify goals, values, and audience needs. • Design the Strategy: Build a tailored plan that resonates and creates impact. • Deliver and Refine: Implement with precision and optimize for results. • Pair this with a CTA like "Let's Get Started" or "Work With Us."
Social Proof & Trust Section	Purpose-led brands thrive on authenticity and trust. Reinforce your credibility by integrating: Testimonials: Real stories from clients who align with your mission. "Their guidance helped us amplify our message and connect authentically with our audience." Partnerships and Certifications: Feature collaborations, sustainability certifications, or awards that showcase your values. Impact Metrics: Highlight measurable successes, such as audience growth, engagement, or community impact.

Messaging Recipe for An Effective HomePage	
Invitation to Learn More Section	Towards the bottom of your homepage, give your audience a path to learn more, guiding them to other parts of your website. You might, for example, feature and/or link to • Case studies or success stories. • Blog or insights pages with thought leadership content. • Contact page or form, with a simple CTA like "Let's Talk."

Customizing Your Recipes

The recipes above are yours to modify in any way you choose. You can remove any irrelevant questions, add, subtract, or modify sections, and add in questions that you need answers to. One row I often add to any product or service marketing recipe for clients, for example, is an Evidence or Examples row. To tell a story well, you're going to need to provide evidence of how it works and/or the value you provide. You don't need to include full-text case studies in your recipe, but just have a think in advance about WHICH case studies, testimonials, data, or examples you might draw on in your marketing that will best demonstrate the effectiveness of your product or solution.

For old former journalists like me, even just completing the above exercises generates a slew of content ideas for web copy, blog content, and social posts.

Next, let's look at how to organize them all into a coherent and effective content plan.

"Good content
isn't about
good storytelling.
It's about telling a
true story well."

~ ANN HANDLEY

CHAPTER 10

CREATING AN ON-MESSAGE CONTENT PLAN

If you've begun working on the suggested exercises in this book, I'm betting that you're starting to have a good idea of the kinds of things you need to say to gain the attention and trust of your audience. You might even have a few usable messaging recipes to use in your content. Huzzah! Give yourself a big ol' pat on the back.

The next challenge for you as a communicator will be applying it to actual content. Happily, this chapter presents a straightforward game plan. To be more specific, we'll work now on developing a super-simple Content Plan for your brand that's guided by the messaging you've thoughtfully developed to date. And because that messaging stems from your Purpose Statement and Core Brand Messaging, you can be assured that it's also rooted in your values and purpose.

A proviso: This is not a full content marketing strategy or roadmap. And you'll likely have a lot of work to do tactically and operationally to sort out how you're going to execute everything. That's the subject matter for a future book. But it will give you an on-point, on-brand plan for your next few months of content.

To create your unique content plan, you'll need to develop the following in sequence:

- Story Pillars
- Key Themes
- Content Formats
- Story Ideas

Step One: Define Your Story Pillars

Your first step is all about organizing your thoughts. One of the first ways that our agency team learned to translate a client's key messaging into actionable content was to use the structure of Story Pillars (sometimes also called content pillars).

No matter what you choose to call them, think of Story Pillars as your main 'content buckets.' They should represent the subject matter, ideas, themes, and topics around which you, your business, or brand most want to create content.

By taking the time to identify and then prioritize your content pillars, you'll be able to figure out:

- Where you and your team most want to be seen as an authority or expert
- The main topics you want to write or talk about in your content
- Which topics will allow you to meet your content OKRs

We often do an exercise with new clients where we ask them to—using a Miro board—simply brainstorm all the things they want to talk about in their content. It's an absurdly simple yet remarkably effective way to get to the bottom of what a group of people really wants to communicate about a brand. And you know what? Story pillars are surprisingly consistent across our clients. That's because, in a broad sense, we all—as brands or businesses—need to tell the same kinds of stories to build trust and authority.

Below, I've gathered the most commonly applied Story Pillars we work with. As you review each, note that I recommend working with no more than three pillars at a time.

Value Stories: Stories that help to express the key values of the brand and show how the company or leader truly lives them. Stories told within this pillar include transparency stories, ethics stories, employee well-being stories, sustainability stories, corporate responsibility stories, and so on.

Cause Stories: A slight offshoot from the values pillar, cause stories tend to be more specifically devoted to promoting a particular belief, cause, or drive for change that your brand is closely aligned with. An example might be Ben & Jerry's, a brand that's extremely vocal about their support for social and political causes such as LGBTQ+ rights, racial justice, and climate action. They often use their marketing platforms (website, social content) to discuss such issues and advocate for change.

Customer/Audience Success Stories: These kinds of stories emotionally show how the audience achieves success of some kind (solving a problem, overcoming an obstacle, achieving fabulous results) because of the solution you're offering. Warby Parker's content marketing strategy uses customer stories as a fundamental pillar, evident in their "Wearing Warby" blog series, which contains customer stories galore.

Company Success Stories: Public companies needing to build trust among potential and/or current shareholders tend to focus on sharing news about their growth, stability, and success to inspire trust and confidence. A slightly surprising example is Etsy, a brand that often shares stories about their growth, financial performance, and success in empowering small businesses and creative entrepreneurs. These stories help build trust and confidence among shareholders and the public.

Product/Service Success Stories: If it's a priority to demonstrate that your product or service makes a real difference to your customers' lives, then this should be a pillar. Fine-tune it so that you're not talking about success broadly but rather homing in on a few specific successes or transformations that you prompt. See how your transformation messaging comes into play here?

Relationship/Partnership Stories: If an alliance, partnership, or collaboration is central to your brand story, shout that story from the rooftop—warts and all. People understand the value of working together, as well as how tough it can be. These are the kinds of stories that have a natural arc, involve people with all their complexities, and that people really relate to on an emotional level.

Stories About Your Industry: These kinds of stories can demonstrate your knowledge of your industry and how you stand out within it. New Belgium Brewing, a craft beer company, often shares stories about the brewing industry, beer culture, and how they're innovating and pushing boundaries within the craft beer space.

Stories About Your Brand or History: These stories tend to showcase a company's founding story to capture a little of its spirit, heritage, values, and mission. Stonyfield Organic is a great example of this kind of storytelling. They effectively share stories about their founding and growth, emphasizing their commitment to organic agriculture and sustainable business practices since founding, all to express the spirit and mission behind the brand.

Do any of the pillars above resonate with you for your brand? And how might you use the work you've done on your messaging to help you figure yours out?

Take Note: Story pillars are not objectives—and they're not topics, either!

In content marketing lore, you'll hear a LOT about the need to inspire, educate, entertain, and/or convince. Perhaps some other verbs are thrown in there, too. The 'matrix' was originally conceived by Smart Insights to identify some of the key objectives for your content. In their matrix, content should either entertain, educate, inspire, or convince—depending on where your audience is at in your content funnel, and what your Content Objectives are.

This is a great way to home in on what you want your content to do. But these aren't your pillars.

Your pillars also are not necessarily your content topics, although they can encompass the topics and subjects you write about. You'll tackle those next, in subtopics.

Think of your pillars as umbrella categories—or, again, 'buckets'—that can organize your content planning and creation. They encompass the kinds of content and the topics for content, too, that you're going to write about. They're the broad categories that should provide both focus and structure for your content creation.

How to Identify _Your_ Pillars

Review your key messages and recipes to date and look at the key messages you've developed. Your messages will likely translate into broader themes that can serve as your Story Pillars. For example, if a critical message emphasizes sustainability, one of the Story Pillars could be environmental stewardship.

Return to your purpose and core values: These elements highlight what your brand stands for. Are there stories you can or should tell that express or reflect this?

Align with your audience's needs: Consider your audience's pain points, challenges, and aspirations, as identified in the messaging framework. Story pillars should address these aspects, creating narratives that resonate with the audience and position the brand as a solution or partner in their journey.

Reflect on what makes you different: If you need to highlight what sets your brand apart from competitors, a story pillar could reinforce these differentiators, helping you to stand out in the market by consistently telling stories that showcase its unique strengths and approach.

Hot AI Prompt: Defining Your Story Pillars

"Story pillars are an excellent way to translate a brand's key messaging into actionable content. Story pillars are a brand's main 'content buckets.' They should represent the subject matter, ideas, themes and topics around which you, your business, or your brand most want to create content. Given this, please identify what [Your Brand]'s three Story Pillars are based on our website."

Step Two: Get Clear on Your 'Themes' Within Each Pillar

Within each story pillar, you'll have much to say. You'll want to share examples, information, opinions, and to tell stories about certain things, which we classify as themes.

Themes are the essence of each story pillar, crafted as meaningful, memorable statements that express your brand's beliefs, commitments, and unique contributions. They unify what you stand for with what you want your audience to feel and understand about your brand. Themes connect purpose to audience values, helping to build a consistent, impactful message across all channels.

When you identify the key themes for each of your Story Pillars, consider—honestly—the kinds of things you tell your team, your customers, and partners regularly. What types of things have these folks heard a million times from you?

For me, that's easy. My team hears me regularly saying things like ...

- If a piece of our content sounds like something anybody else could write or produce, it needs more work. It needs to sound uniquely like us / the brand we're supporting.
- No typos or grammatical errors, ever!
- At least two pairs of eyes on every piece of content, always!

These are all my themes, if you will, that, when applied to our marketing, speak to our more significant stories about our commitment to quality and authenticity.

How to Define _Your_ Themes

Root in Core Beliefs: Start by identifying what drives your brand's purpose beyond profit, speaking directly to the mission and ideals that guide your work.

Align with Audience Values: Every theme should clearly resonate with what matters to your audience. Consider what they value in brands like yours, and reflect these ideals in language that speaks to shared goals and commitments.

Craft for Clarity and Impact: Keep themes short and powerful, aiming to capture your brand's core messaging in a memorable, unified statement that feels authentic and unique to your brand.

Ensure Consistency: Themes should be flexible enough to apply across formats and channels while consistently reinforcing the brand's purpose and values.

Incorporate Action and Aspiration: Infuse each theme with a sense of purpose-driven momentum. Use language that suggests active, intentional engagement in creating a positive impact.

By using themes in this way, you ensure that each pillar expresses your brand's identity meaningfully while staying aligned with audience values, helping to foster trust and long-term engagement.

Step Three: Choose Content Formats That Best Tell Your Story

Choosing the right content formats is an essential step in connecting with your audience and achieving your goals. The key lies in understanding who you're speaking to, the nature of your message, and how these align with your broader strategy.

How to Choose *Your* Content Formats

Let's go back to your audience. Knowing who these folks are, what they value, and how they consume content is crucial. Different formats resonate with different demographics. For example, younger audiences might engage more with short-form video content or interactive social posts, while B2B professionals may prefer in-depth whitepapers, reports, or webinars. Tools like Google Analytics, audience surveys, and social listening can provide insights into the formats that your audience prefers. Ann Handley, a respected voice in content marketing, emphasizes that understanding your audience's needs and habits is foundational to choosing the right formats.

Next, consider the message you want to convey. The formats you choose should complement your content rather than limit it. If you need to explain something complex, for example, long-form content like blog posts, eBooks, or infographics might be your best bet, as they allow for depth and clarity. For quick updates or engaging on-the-go audiences, shorter formats like tweets, Instagram stories, or bite-sized videos are more effective. Content strategist Jay Baer reminds us that the format should serve the content rather than the other way around.

Finally, align your format choices with your overall content strategy. If building authority in your industry is your goal, then long-form, research-driven content such as case studies or whitepapers will be crucial. But if you're aiming for brand awareness and reach, shareable formats like videos, infographics, or even podcasts might be more effective. Consistency across different formats is also key—it helps create a cohesive brand experience that meets your audience where they are while reinforcing your message across all channels.

Formats to Consider

Blogs/Articles: Longer-form content that offers valuable insights, tips, and stories to your audience.

Videos: Videos can be used for a range of purposes, including brand storytelling, education, demonstrating your product or service, sharing insights, capturing customer insights/reviews, and offering behind-the-scenes glimpses of who you are and what you do.

Social Media Posts: Updates and posts on platforms like Facebook, Instagram, Twitter, LinkedIn, and TikTok that can highlight your brand values, initiatives, knowledge, and insights or showcase your values, impact, and community involvement.

Infographics: Visual representations of data, statistics, or processes related to your results, purpose, or industry, designed to be easily shareable and digestible.

Podcasts: Audio content featuring interviews, discussions, or stories related to your mission, values, and industry topics.

Webinars: Live or pre-recorded online seminars or workshops that educate and engage audiences on relevant topics related to the brand's purpose and offerings.

Case Studies: Generally in-depth analyses of successful projects, services, partnerships, or initiatives intended to showcase or detail the kind of impact your brand has had and how you've lived out your purpose.

Email Newsletters: Regular updates sent to subscribers' inboxes, featuring curated content, product updates, and stories aligned with the brand's purpose.

User-Generated Content (UGC): This is content created by customers or followers, such as reviews, testimonials, or photos, showcasing their experiences with the brand and its products.

Interactive Content: Engaging experiences like quizzes, polls, surveys, or interactive maps that encourage audience participation and feedback.

Whitepapers/eBooks: These are generally helpful and sometimes comprehensive documents that explore industry trends, research findings, or best practices, showcasing your brand's expertise and thought leadership.

Live Streams: Real-time video broadcasts on platforms like Facebook Live, Instagram Live, or YouTube Live, featuring events, interviews, or behind-the-scenes moments.

Virtual Events: Online events, conferences, or workshops that bring together like-minded individuals to discuss topics related to the brand's purpose and industry.

Community Forums: Online platforms or groups where customers and followers can connect, share ideas, and discuss topics relevant to the brand's purpose.

Animations/GIFs: Short, animated clips or graphics that convey messages, evoke emotions, or explain concepts related to the brand's purpose and offerings.

Collaborations: Partnerships with influencers, other brands, or organizations to co-create content and amplify messaging related to shared values and initiatives.

Visual Stories: Sequenced images or videos on platforms like Instagram Stories or Snapchat, showcasing behind-the-scenes moments, product features, or user-generated content.

Augmented Reality (AR) Experiences: Interactive digital overlays or filters allow users to engage creatively and effectively with the brand's purpose or products.

Interactive Maps: Visual representations of the brand's impact, reach, or initiatives, allowing users to explore and interact with relevant locations or data points.

Microsites/Landing Pages: Dedicated web pages or mini-sites that focus on specific campaigns, causes, or initiatives related to the brand's purpose, with clear calls to action for engagement or donations.

Step Four: Capture Story Ideas for Each Pillar

Now that you've identified your Story Pillars, themes, and formats, it's time to get specific. This is where the fun starts: brainstorming individual stories that bring each of your pillars to life. With a thoughtful approach, you can generate story ideas that convey the full depth of your brand's purpose while engaging audiences at every level. Let's look at how to create stories that will resonate, using macro and micro storytelling.

Macro Storytelling (Long-Form Content)

Think of macro storytelling as the big-picture, deep-dive content that allows you to fully explore a theme within your pillar. This might take the form of blog posts, in-depth articles, or whitepapers. Each piece should express a key aspect of your brand's purpose, values, or expertise.

To generate macro-story ideas, start with your themes. Look at each theme within a pillar and ask questions like:

- What is the broader story here?

- What specific questions or challenges does my audience have around this topic?

- How can I add value by exploring a key opinion or position?

For example, in Forge & Spark's Purpose & Impact pillar, a macro-story might be an in-depth blog post on "Why Purpose-Led Brands Drive Positive Change" or a case study showing how a client amplified its impact by collaborating with Forge & Spark.

Tip: Capture ideas continuously by keeping a dedicated space for brainstorming—Slack, a notes app, or an idea board. Our team at Forge & Spark regularly jots down ideas in a shared Slack channel, then pulls the best ones into our content calendar during planning sessions.

Once you have a macro-story idea, you can then create a content brief that includes:

- SEO keywords: To boost discoverability.

- Target audience: Define who will benefit most from this story.

- Ideal action: Identify what you want readers to do after engaging.

- Story structure: Use a clear introduction, a well-structured body, and a conclusion to guide the reader.

Macro stories should be rich in information and detail, and—to ensure that they stand out from the sea of generic stories out there—must include elements like:

- Personal anecdotes or case studies: stories within the story that show personality and perspective.

- Evidence, data or statistics that back up the points you're making and add further colour

- Quotes to lend authority, perspective and further personality

- Visuals like infographics or photos to not only break up text but also to add interest and further personality

Micro Storytelling (Social & Short-Form Content)

Micro storytelling involves creating shorter, more immediate stories that distill your brand's message into bite-sized content pieces. These might include social media posts, quick reels, or even short email updates that allow you to share highlights and build a consistent presence.

With micro-stories, you'll take elements from your macro-stories (like a compelling quote, a key stat, or a testimonial) and turn them into standalone pieces that can be easily shared across platforms.

Here are a couple of ways to develop micro-story ideas:

- Focus on one impactful detail or key point: Pull out a striking statistic, engaging customer quote, or behind-the-scenes moment to share on social media. You might also home in on one key point (from a bullet list like this).

- Use on-brand visuals for impact: A compelling image can emotionally engage and communicate your story's essence. Pull out the same one used in your macro-story, and use the caption to add a new personal take, or to tag someone mentioned in the story and celebrate their part in it.

For example, Forge & Spark's Focus on Quality pillar has inspired micro-story series on Instagram featuring visually rich carousels highlighting some of the quality work we produce for individual clients, and plenty of testimonial posts from satisfied clients who, in their words, speak to our emphasis on quality.

How to Capture *Your* Story Ideas

Developing ideas for each content pillar is where strategy meets creativity. Here's how to make the process manageable and keep ideas flowing:

Brainstorm and Capture: Block out time each month to brainstorm story ideas for each pillar, with a goal of generating at least three ideas per pillar (one long-form, one social, and one video or personal note). Use collaborative tools, such as Slack or Miro, where team members can drop in ideas as they come up.

Organize and Prioritize: Regularly review your captured ideas and pull the best ones into your content plan. Forge & Spark's content team, for example, meets monthly to review and select ideas that align with the brand's current priorities and client projects.

Brief, Outline, and Develop: For each go-ahead story idea, create a brief that includes SEO keywords, audience, and a call to action. Outline the story structure to keep the content focused and effective.

Iterate and Refine: As you publish and receive feedback on your content, revisit your ideas and briefs. See what resonates most with your audience and adjust accordingly. Micro-content, in particular, can be a testing ground for new ideas that might evolve into larger stories later on.

Putting It All Together

With a variety of stories inspired by each of your pillars, you can readily create a cohesive, on-brand content plan that reflects your brand's values while engaging your audience across different channels and touchpoints.

When you try out the various stories and formats, take care to see what works best. Report monthly on your content guided by your OKRs, taking note of the stories and formats that deliver your best (and worst) results. Informed by data, you can then adjust your content mix to ensure that your content reaches your audience, builds a lasting connection grounded in purpose and trust, *and* achieves business results.

A Fictional Example: Smart Snacks' Pillars, Themes & Formats

To illustrate the outcome of the process I've described above, I've drawn it all together for a fictional brand, which I've called Smart Snacks, to show how a well-rounded content plan comes to life when we align Story Pillars, themes, formats, and story ideas.

I began by identifying a few promising Story Pillars for SmartCrackers, a company that sustainably produces organic crackers that also taste delicious. They include:

- **Sustainability:** All the ways the company goes above and beyond, including ethical sourcing, packaging, and considerations for the supply chain. Always consider what the audience cares about in terms of sustainability, too.

- **Social Impact / Values:** This pillar might tell stories about the brand or founder's purpose, zeroing in on a particular focus (like social impact or community)

- **Health & Well-Being:** These are healthy crackers, right? There are a multitude of stories about health and wellness that might be told to really let the audience know the key benefits of the product.

Here's how we might outline the corresponding themes, and content formats, for this example.

Pillar 1: Sustainability

This pillar highlights Smart Snacks' commitment to ethical sourcing, sustainable production, and eco-friendly packaging, reflecting the brand's core dedication to environmental stewardship and transparency.

Messaging Themes:

- "Ethically nourishing the world, one cracker at a time."

- "From our farms to your table, protecting the planet every step of the way."

- "Transparency and responsibility in every bite."

Content Formats:

- **Farm-to-Table Stories:** Long-form blog posts or video documentaries tracing ingredients from their origin to the final product, showcasing the farmers and sustainable practices involved

- **Sustainable Packaging Spotlights:** Visual content such as infographics or video series highlighting the lifecycle of the brand's eco-friendly packaging

- **Supply Chain Transparency Features:** Profile stories and behind-the-scenes visuals of supply chain partners to build trust and reinforce Smart Snacks' ethical sourcing practices

Story Ideas:

- *Roots to Ritz: A Cracker's Journey from Farm to Table*

  - ☐ **Format**: Blog post or documentary-style video

  - ☐ **Description**: Trace the journey of a Smart Snacks cracker from farm to table, with interviews and insights from the farmers who supply the ingredients, showing the impact of sustainable farming

- *Packaging with a Purpose: How Our Eco-Friendly Boxes are Saving Trees*

  - ☐ **Format**: Fun, informative short video series

  - ☐ **Description**: Use short, engaging videos to showcase unique features of the eco-friendly packaging, from biodegradable materials to innovative designs that align with the brand's sustainability values

- *Seeing Is Believing: A Virtual Tour of Our Transparent Supply Chain*

  - ☐ **Format**: Interactive web experience or virtual tour video

  - ☐ **Description**: A virtual tour that gives audiences a firsthand look at the operations and partners behind Smart Snacks, fostering transparency and credibility

Pillar 2: Social Impact & Values

In this pillar, Smart Snacks emphasizes its commitment to community engagement, inclusivity, and positive social impact, supporting local initiatives and giving back to its communities.

Messaging Themes:

- "Together, we build stronger communities through food."

- "Rooted in values: for people, for planet, for a purpose."

- "Diversity and inclusivity in every flavor."

Content Formats:

- **Community Impact Stories**: Blog posts or video series covering volunteer events, donations, and partnerships that benefit local communities

- **Diversity Profiles**: Highlighting diverse team members, suppliers, and partners, reinforcing the brand's commitment to inclusivity

- **Collaborations & Partnerships**: Posts or case studies featuring collaborations with community-focused organizations and initiatives aligned with Smart Snacks' mission

Story Ideas:

- *Meet the Makers: Profiles on Our Diverse Team and Suppliers*

  - ☐ **Format**: Photo series or short videos with personal quotes

  - ☐ **Description**: Humanize Smart Snacks by profiling team members and suppliers from diverse backgrounds, sharing their personal stories and values

- *Collaborating for Change: Smart Snacks x Local Food Bank Initiative*

  - ☐ **Format**: Case study or social carousel

  - ☐ **Description**: Highlight a recent partnership with a local food bank, showing how Smart Snacks' contributions and volunteer efforts are impacting the community

- *Celebrating Community Impact: A Monthly Volunteer Day Recap*

  - ☐ **Format**: Short social media videos and blog recap

  - ☐ **Description**: Monthly stories showcasing employee volunteer days, including visuals of team members actively participating in local events to foster community spirit

Pillar 3: Health & Well-Being

This pillar underscores Smart Snacks as a health-conscious brand that supports wellness and promotes balanced lifestyles through its nutritious, wholesome products.

Messaging Themes:

- "Snack well, live well."

- "Fueling bodies and spirits, one wholesome bite at a time."

- "Healthy snacking for a thriving life."

Content Formats:

- **Nutritional Highlights:** Infographics, blog posts, or videos that detail the health benefits of Smart Snacks' ingredients

- **Recipe Inspirations:** Social media posts or videos showcasing creative ways to incorporate Smart Snacks into balanced meals

- **Health & Wellness Tips:** Educational articles or social posts offering wellness advice that aligns with Smart Snacks' commitment to healthy living

Story Ideas:

- *Power Up: Nutritional Benefits of Our Ingredients*

  - ☐ **Format:** Infographic or blog post

  - ☐ **Description:** Highlight the key health benefits of ingredients in Smart Snacks, explaining how they support overall wellness and a balanced lifestyle

- *Smart Snacks Recipe Challenge: Inspiring New Ways to Enjoy Healthy Snacking*

- [ ] **Format**: Social media series or campaign featuring user-generated content

- [ ] **Description**: Invite followers to share their favorite ways to use Smart Snacks in meals, fostering a community-driven collection of recipe ideas

- *Snack Smarter: Wellness Tips for a Healthier, Happier Life*

  - [ ] **Format**: Blog post or short video series

  - [ ] **Description**: Practical wellness advice that aligns with Smart Snacks' brand values, covering topics like mindful eating, balanced snacking, and more

With each pillar, theme, and content format fully defined, our fictional brand Smart Snacks has a blueprint they might use to plan, develop, and deliver a range of content aligned with its mission that delivers results.

Putting Vapour to Paper

You're probably reading this book because you have a kajillion ideas for content and things you want to say. However, you may have had difficulty translating those airy concepts into content and communication that feels right. Am I right?

So, here's where the rubber hits the road. Or, as my B Corp guides at Decade Impact kept putting it when my team was seeking certification: *Vapour to paper, Shannon!* Get that stuff out of your head and document it. Somewhere. Anywhere!

A Sample Content Plan for Forge & Spark

Here's another example, from our own planning, to illustrate how pillars, themes, content formats, and story ideas, can come together in a plan designed to express our core brand messaging in content that drives results.

Pillar 1: Purpose & Impact

In this pillar, we highlight our commitment to working with purpose-led brands and leaders who prioritize making a positive difference, and celebrate those brands and their impact through a lens of authentic content marketing and communication.

Messaging Themes:

- Let's value and celebrate the commitment of all those making a positive impact in the world.

- Content can be an excellent medium for celebrating and extending the influence of purpose-led leaders and brands.

- Earning trust with customers starts with authenticity and clarity in communications.

Content Formats:

- **Case Studies & Blog Posts**: In-depth stories of how Forge & Spark has helped brands define and communicate their purpose.

- **Social Conversations & Engagement**: Interactive posts and polls on platforms like LinkedIn or Instagram focused on purpose in leadership and content.

- **Client Appreciation Series**: Posts and videos celebrating clients' purpose and successes.

- **Educational Articles**: Informative pieces about effective purpose-led leadership in content.

- **Amplification Posts**: Social media highlights that share and support client achievements.

Pillar 2: Focus on Quality

Quality content is essential to reflect the overall quality and credibility of a brand. In this pillar, we emphasize that thoughtfulness, visual impact, and impeccable writing are critical elements of content that align with a brand's purpose and values.

Messaging Themes:

- **Thoughtfulness & Craftsmanship:** Content quality—in everything from messaging to visual impact to writing—can express a brand's best qualities

- **Impact:** Quality content isn't just seen; it's felt and remembered.

- **Strategy is Consistency:** Thoughtful strategy delivers the right content in the right ways for your brand, consistently across channels.

Content Formats:

- **Thought Leadership Articles:** Pieces on the relationship between authenticity and successful marketing.

- **Visual Showcases:** Posts highlighting examples of high-quality content with explanations of what makes them stand out.

- **Educational Reels:** Short videos from team members sharing insights into creating authentic, impactful content.

- **Spotlight Stories:** Highlighting why specific content Forge & Spark finds inspirational is exemplary.

Pillar 3: Us & Our Work

This pillar highlights Forge & Spark's team, showing who we are so that potential clients can evaluate us, and current clients feel proud to work with us. We emphasize our collaborative spirit, and the authentic, human-centered approach we bring to their work.

Messaging Themes:

- Our team represents a balance of personal passion, professional expertise, and experience.

- We're a true partner to our clients—often for the long term—and care about that relationship.

- We're warm and fun to work with.

Content Formats

- **Behind-the-Scenes Videos**: Quick snapshots of team meetings, brainstorming sessions, and fun moments.

- **Case Studies & Problem-Solving Posts**: In-depth analyses of specific projects, focusing on problem-solving and successful outcomes.

- **Client Love Posts:** Shout-outs and stories showcasing projects, detailing what was done and celebrating the client's impact.

- **Educational Series:** Content pieces from team members sharing their learnings, tools, and tips.

- **Future: Interactive Q&A Sessions & Webinars:** Live social media sessions or stories to engage with audiences and share expertise.

Making Your Plan Actionable

And here, at last, is where it all gets ridiculously actionable. You know what you want to cover in your content (pillars). You know what you want to say (themes). You've identified a few ways to express your ideas (formats). And you've even got a few starter story ideas.

To make your plan actionable, ensure that it's realistic. Consider what you and your team can reasonably produce in a given month or quarter that:

a) Help you make progress against your OKRs

b) Speak to your personas

c) Express each of your Story Pillars and various themes

And please remember that you don't have to do everything right away. Give yourself space and grace, and take it slowly if you need to, giving you and your team a chance to iterate: try something, see how it works, and improve it as needed—or lose it forever if it proved either impractical (too hard to produce consistently) or didn't meet your objectives.

A Sample Plan for a Month of Content

Here's one way to organize your plan, ensuring a balance of content formats and pillars. To ensure practicality, consider tackling just one format per month at a time, and add to your content volume slowly over time, once you get that first piece just right.

Balance macro-content with micro-content. The simplest way to think about this is: for every article, blog, case study, or video you produce (that's your macro-content), try to come up with three social posts (micro-content) that each express one of your Story Pillars.

Simple Plan Example - Monthly Content Overview

- **Primary Content Anchor:** One blog post or LinkedIn article about a topic that both engages or helps your audience, and that drives to one of your OKRs

- **Supporting Content:** One simple social media post and one short video to tell the same story as micro-content

As one example, that could translate into one thoughtful LinkedIn article or blog post about, say, the importance of quality content marketing. Once you've created that piece of macro-content (and know it's driving the right action to help you meet your OKRs), you can then consider some of the supporting content you can produce to ensure that this story captures the attention of, and offers value to, folks on your other channels, too. That might—as a start—simply mean shooting a short video where you discuss an idea in your article or blog post, Or it could mean drafting a simple post for a channel like Instagram, using your blog image and a short caption that captures an idea shared in your blog. Right there, you've got a solid piece of anchor content that you can keep promoting (and updating, then re-promoting) over time, plus two social posts. This is an excellent start to effective, and on-purpose content marketing!

Robust Plan Example - Monthly Content Overview

From the simple example, you'll see that a good content plan begins with a story designed to serve both your audience (delivering value and appeal) and you, too (helping you achieve your Content Objectives). Tell it as both a macro-story (a blog, an article or essay, or a video) and as at least one micro-story on your social channels. This is the simplest version of what I call a story package.

Incrementally adding to your monthly content plan can then be as easy as increasing the number of items in one story package, or increasing the number and type of story packages you produce.

Once you've got that content rolling and delivering results, you can add to your plan further by introducing more standalone social content items: posts and stories that *aren't* necessarily tied to a piece of macro-content, but that still express one or more of your Story Pillars and themes. Here's what a robust plan including all of these elements might look like:

- **Two Content Anchors:** One long-form blog post + one case study (either new or updated)

- **Supporting Content:** For each anchor, include 2-3 social media posts, videos, or stories (ideally covering a range of your Story Pillars)

- **Standalone, Engagement-focused Social Content:** Weekly posts touching on each of your Story Pillars. If your story packages aren't expressing all of your Story Pillars, use standalone social content to capture them. Examples might be posts, behind-the-scenes glimpses of you and your team, and re-posts of your clients' successes or wins that can help humanize the brand and showcase expertise.

Here's how to flesh out this robust plan in more detail, using specific story examples from Forge & Spark.

Macro-Content #1 - Blog-Based Story Package

Content Output: 1 long-form blog post + 3 social media posts that can be used across channels (e.g., LinkedIn, Instagram, Facebook, X).

Anchor Blog Theme: Thought leadership on how content quality helps to build brand trust and authenticity. Ties into our "Focus on Quality" pillar.

Social Media Posts:

- **LinkedIn Highlight**: A brief overview with insights from the blog, focusing on why quality content fosters long-term trust

- **Instagram Visual Excerpt**: A carousel post featuring key takeaways presented with visual appeal
- **Wildcard Post:** A behind-the-scenes insight into Forge & Spark's process for ensuring top-tier content quality, showcasing team dedication.

Macro-Content #2 - Case Study-Based Story Package

Content Output: 1 case study + 3 social media posts (LinkedIn, Instagram, Facebook, X).

Case Study Focus: Showcase a recent project with a purpose-driven client, demonstrating impactful results and client collaboration. Aligns with the "Purpose & Impact" and "Us & Our Work" pillars.

Social Media Posts:

- **Client Celebration**: A post highlighting the client's journey and the collaborative success, with visuals showing before-and-after results
- **Results Highlight**: A post emphasizing key outcomes and value, underlining Forge & Spark's expertise
- **Testimonial Post:** A quote from the client praising the collaboration and results achieved

Standalone Micro-Content: Social Posts & Stories

Content Output: 4 varied social media posts for engagement.

Pillars Covered: Purpose & Impact, Focus on Quality, Us & Our Work.

Types of Posts:

- **Values-Rich Post:** An update on Forge & Spark's commitment to a sustainability initiative or B Corp-related cause

- **Client Love:** A spotlight post celebrating a client's milestone or resharing a client success story that resonates with Forge & Spark's mission (this could be different than the social post promoting the case study)

- **Expertise Post:** An educational reel featuring quick tips on creating authentic, impactful content

- **Team Highlight:** A casual video or photo showcasing team collaboration or a moment from a content brainstorming session, building the "Us & Our Work" narrative

What This Looks Like on a Calendar

Week One

Focus: Macro-Content #1 - Blog-Based Story Package

- **Monday:** Publish your long-form blog post about "How content quality builds brand trust and authenticity"

- **Wednesday:** Have the author of the post share a LinkedIn highlight post summarizing the blog's key insights, then repost it from your brand account

- **Friday:** Create and post an Instagram carousel with visual takeaways from the blog

Week Two

Focus: Macro-Content #1 - Supporting Content & Engagement

- **Tuesday:** Create a post *not* related to the blog, expressing a different story pillar: a pic, perhaps, showcasing the team or values

- **Thursday:** Repurpose the blog post for an email newsletter, creating a teaser to drive traffic back to the blog.

- **Friday**: Share an engagement-driven post on social such as a question relating to the blog (e.g., "What do you think makes content trustworthy?") and respond to comments

Week Two

Focus: Macro-Content #2 - Case Study-Based Story Package

- **Monday**: Publish a new or updated case study highlighting a recent project and impactful results

- **Wednesday**: Have the author or a member of your team share a LinkedIn post celebrating the client's success and collaboration, with visuals from the case study ... then have other team members like and comment on it to amplify, including reposting from your company profile

- **Thursday**: Post a results-focused update on Instagram, emphasizing key takeaways from the case study

Week Four

Focus: Standalone, Engagement-Focused Social Content

- **Tuesday**: Create a social post based on a different pillar not covered yet in the month, such as a Values-Rich Post highlighting Forge & Spark's commitment to collaboration

- **Thursday**: Celebrate a client's milestone with a "Client Love" post on Instagram or Facebook

- **Friday**: Share an educational reel with quick tips for creating authentic, impactful content (Expertise Post)

Possible Additions or Trade-Ins

- **Occasional Stories:** Post Instagram or Facebook Stories with quick updates, sneak peeks, polls, or engagement prompts

- **Reposting**: Throughout the month, reshare relevant content from clients or partners that aligns with Forge & Spark's pillars

- **Engaging**: Throughout the month, ensure that you or someone on your team engages with your client or partner content by commenting, liking, or resharing with your own insight or comments

This monthly 'calendar' can most certainly be modified according to your goals, schedule, and energy. I provide it as an example of how you might balance macro-content, micro-content, and standalone social posts while spreading tasks and publication across the month to maintain consistency and engagement—and hopefully your sanity, too.

We most certainly don't adhere to this schedule strictly, but it does guide our monthly content planning. We generally hit our target of publishing highly relevant social content twice weekly, along with two pieces of search-optimized and on-brand long-form content that's closely tied to our business objectives.

Your publishing frequency, the channels you choose, and the kinds of content that work best for your audience are all part of your deeper content marketing strategy and how you set up your operations.

But looking at the example above, I hope that you'll see that—if messaging is indeed a priority for you—you've now got a well-balanced content plan that expresses the kinds of messages you most want to convey. This content plan, grounded in exactly the right messaging, should not only feel like a relief but also a significant achievement.

But Wait ... Does Your Messaging Work?

Ah yes. How do you make sure it's working for you? You will actively need to test and refine your messaging ... Well, forever, actually. And that isn't as scary as it sounds. In fact, armed with the right tactics, you should feel empowered to continuously improve your messaging.

We're learning creatures. We do this constantly in our daily conversations and interactions. We listen to how others are speaking and ask questions. We adjust and adapt our language, tone, and style to meet their needs and preferences or simply make them feel comfortable. This is what I'm talking about: tweaking your language, adjusting your wording, and emphasizing one thing over another because it's landing better for your audience. Remember, your ability to adapt and learn from your audience should be a source of reassurance.

Here are a few tactics you might consider.

Ongoing Measurement Against OKRS

The good news is that you've already done the hard work of defining your objectives and prioritizing the results that are most important to you. When you know what you're trying to accomplish—whether increasing brand awareness, driving conversions, enriching your relationship with existing customers or audiences, or another objective—you can measure progress against that. Reporting against those KPIs we identified back in Chapter 5 will quickly show you how your messaging is doing in terms of achieving those cold, hard results.

Gauge Your Messaging With Your Audience: Measure Engagement and Ask Them

Aha! More good news: You already know well the audience you're trying to engage with your content. You 'get' what they want to accomplish (JTBD), you feel their pain points, and you know (or will get to know) their demographics, psychographics, and preferences. When you do your reporting, don't forget to regularly report on how your audience is growing, changing, and evolving and which kinds of content pieces are resonating most with them. Don't hesitate to evolve your personas over time to guide your messaging efforts and—conversely—to tailor your messaging to resonate with different segments of your audience. If a piece of content hits, for example, with a particular persona or demographic, play with it—do more of it! Try different formats. Make it a staple in your marketing.

Test Variations of Your Messaging

If you're in marketing, you know A/B Testing. It's a method of comparing two versions of a webpage or app against each other to determine which one performs better. Try it. A/B testing lets you compare two variations of a message, right down to the wording, to determine which performs better. You can use A/B testing to learn a ton about headlines, story angles, calls-to-action, and so much more. Keep iterating based on your insights.

Don't forget to look at multi-channel testing, too. Although not as conclusive as A/B testing, you should be able to see how various messaging performs across channels, from your website copy to individual social media channels to newsletters and ads. Different channels WILL require different messaging approaches, so pay attention to how your audience engages with content on each platform.

Adjust Your Messaging

Just to underline the point ... You developed your initial messaging based on what you knew or believed. Are you beginning to hear or learn that your audience wants to hear something else? Is your messaging not connecting or yielding results? Don't be afraid to change and evolve your messaging based on what you're learning from them about the kind of language, tone, subject areas, and emotional pay-off that resonates most with them and that makes them take action.

Listen to Your Audience!

Engagement is a fabulous thing to generate within social media, but it doesn't end with watching your engagement stats soar. When your audience is engaging, they're speaking to you. Pay attention to their comments and what they're saying, whether they're saying it directly to you (we often hear from clients directly, for example, about content items that they really love) or via social media interactions. You might even try surveys or social polls from time to time to ask your audience what is hitting—and what might be missing completely. Then, once you've listened, remember to respond (preferably like a human person and not just a marketer).

Beginners' Mind

What you know now might feel like a lot. Amazing. Just be prepared to be wrong somewhere down the road, with the understanding that this is all part of the journey. Marketing messaging is an ongoing process of wins and misses, humbly learning lessons, and adjusting your approach, just to try it out all over again. Stay humble, stay open, and keep being willing to learn.

Most Importantly, Ensure It's Authentic

Please remember that data only gets you so far. While testing your messaging, please don't forget to gauge it against your brand purpose, values, mission, vision, essence, and, just as importantly, your gut. Does it feel right? Does it feel like you? Like nobody else could say exactly what you're saying, how you're saying it?

If so, you're precisely where you need to be. Congratulations.

CONCLUSION: THE IMPACT OF AUTHENTICITY

In my career, I've relied more on my intuition than on any traditional playbook—because the conventional routes didn't feel right for me. This approach has yielded its fair share of mistakes. It's also taught me invaluable lessons about respecting myself, paying attention, and speaking up (and out) when it matters.

I firmly believe that your unique expression matters, whether you're a junior marketer, a new business owner, or an established veteran. I matter. You matter. The brands and businesses we create matter because there are deeper reasons for bringing them into being. Businesses can be bloody painful to run and keep alive, and yet, most often, we run them with a sense of purpose, which, when clarified, can fuel us and our teams to use that business as a force for good.

I've spent a good chunk of time being a student of communication and connection, learning how content can help purpose-led businesses grow. I am always trying to get to the heart of what makes our communication with one another and our connection as brands with audiences genuinely meaningful. Here's what I've learned: It's far less about the grand statements, bold proclamations, or getting your wording perfect than about the sincere, small, and genuine moments that resonate deeply with those we aim to reach and the cumulative impact of how you express what and who you are.

This book explores lessons and examples from brands that masterfully blend their purpose with their marketing. It's clear now, more than ever, that authentic marketing thrives on narratives that aim for business success and aspire to foster meaningful change. These narratives aren't just stories; they're testaments to the transformative potential of marketing that's rooted in purpose.

Grounded Marketing & Messaging

As I hope I've conveyed, the key to my particular methodology for genuine and authentic marketing messaging lies in clarity about your 'why' and your 'who': your OKRs and your audience personas. After all, as I often say, you need to understand what you most want to accomplish and who you need to get there before you can fine-tune what to say and how to say it to make it all happen.

Defining your OKRs will help you ground your messaging in something far more substantial than vanity metrics. It's about cultivating measurable key results that genuinely reflect the change we—as purpose-driven brands and leaders—aspire to create. This includes things like genuine engagement, brand loyalty, and the strength of our communities. These are the beacons that guide us toward not just quantifiable success but toward making a meaningful difference in the lives of our audience and in the world at large.

And, of course, at the heart of every impactful marketing strategy lies a deep understanding of our audiences. Broad strokes and assumptions aren't going to cut it. Instead, to create significant content for real people, we need to interrogate who those people are, what they most want to accomplish, what they're struggling most with (in the context of what we offer or provide), and how they want to feel. I see this process as a practice in empathy and connection—that subsequently allows us to tailor our messages and strategies in ways that resonate on a deeply personal level, fostering a connection that transcends the transactional.

We're not just shouting into the void by grounding our strategies in Objectives and Key Results (OKRs) that align with our purpose and understanding our audience through detailed personas. Instead, we're engaging in a dialogue that's informed, intentional, and infused with the values that define us.

"Communication is merely an exchange of information, but connection is an exchange of our humanity."

SEAN STEPHENSON

The Imperative of Authenticity

Authenticity is having a moment, for good reason. People are turned off by overly polished or 'cookie-cutter' marketing, and have learned to quickly spot inauthenticity. Transparency is expected; consumers want brands to be open about who they are, what they value, and what they're doing to make an impact. This expectation is especially high among younger generations, like Gen Z and Gen Alpha, who place a premium on authenticity and are drawn to brands that share their values and offer up real and relatable content that tells a brand's true story.

Finding your true voice has always been important on a personal level, and throughout this book you've seen that it's just as essential when it comes to finding and expressing the voice and heart of your brand.

Authenticity can be the foundation of any marketing strategy that seeks to create genuine, lasting relationships rather than fleeting transactions. It can be found in a clear definition of purpose and values and in the knowledge of what's most important.

As consumer expectations shift under our feet, reminding us that brands are no longer mere providers of goods and services but rather expected to be participants in a larger conversation about societal and environmental issues, we are seeing an actual call to action for brands to step up and show their commitment to more than just profit.

Authenticity in the Age of AI

The critical role of authenticity in marketing has never been more apparent. In a world of skepticism, our ability to communicate with transparency and sincerity is not just an advantage—it's a necessity.

Communicating with empathy and creating genuine and engaging content can build a foundation of trust, enabling companies with a purpose to achieve impact in all kinds of areas, from sustainability to social justice. In short, what we say and how we say it matters. And it matters more than ever to be thoughtful in expressing our beliefs, values, and messages.

As artificial intelligence improves, understanding precisely what you want to express and communicate worldwide becomes more critical. We should, as marketers, be able to use AI tools to create efficiencies in our marketing and content operations. We must, in some cases, stay profitable and thriving. But to ensure that our content sounds unique, true to our values, and human, we must be clear about strategy (including OKRs and personas), messaging framework, messaging recipes, and the kinds of content we wish to produce.

So, Where to Next?

Congratulations are in order. You've just completed this deep line of thinking, and can now begin to take advantage of AI's efficiencies. Your purpose is clear. Your goals are clear. The people you need to reach, engage with, and develop trust and community with are clear. You're clear on what you most need to say.

Now, you can feel grounded and clear, act with confidence, and believe that your brand is having an impact on the world and that you can express it with clarity, power, and purpose.

After reading this book and completing your marketing framework and marketing plan, I hope you'll feel clear-headed and purpose-aligned. I hope that, when faced with your next marketing meeting, you'll have moved from a feeling of uncertainty or even dread when it comes to figuring out the kind of content you want to produce to a sense of pride.

You know who you are and what you stand for. You know what you want to do in the world, from the broader impact you want your business to have to the business results you want to accomplish—so that you can grow and truly thrive.

Now, it's time to express it all because you are unique, you belong, and you matter.

I need to be myself.
I can't be no one else.

LIAM GALLAGHER

RESOURCES

Reminder Definitions

STORY PILLARS / CONTENT PILLARS

In content marketing, **'Story Pillars'** (also referred to as **'content pillars'**) are the foundational themes that support your brand narrative and guide your content strategy. These pillars encapsulate the core aspects of your brand's identity, purpose, values, and messaging. By prioritizing the most critical stories your brand needs to tell, Story Pillars serve as the bedrock for building cohesive and aligned content. They help ensure consistency, relevance, and brand alignment across all content marketing efforts, effectively communicating your story, engaging your audience, and achieving your objectives.

CONTENT TOPICS

Content topics are the specific subject areas you choose to cover. Selecting these topics strategically involves considering your expertise, audience interests and needs, industry trends, brand and business objectives, and SEO insights. Your chosen content topics should guide the creation of various content types, ensuring that your content is relevant, valuable, and engaging to your target audiences. This strategic selection helps deliver content that resonates deeply and supports your overarching Story Pillars.

CONTENT FORMATS / TYPES

Content formats, also called content types, refer to the formats used to create and distribute content across different platforms, aiming to attract, engage, entertain, and drive targeted actions from your audience. Common content types in content marketing include:

- Blog Posts
- Social Media Posts and Stories
- Emails/Newsletters
- Videos
- Podcasts
- Case Studies
- Webinars
- Landing Pages and Lead Magnets (eBooks, Whitepapers)

Each type serves different purposes and can be leveraged to meet specific audience preferences and marketing goals.

MESSAGING THEMES

Messaging themes (sometimes called **content themes**) are the unique perspectives and critical messages that consistently emerge in your content. They reflect your brand's unique viewpoints and should be evident across all content you create. Carefully selected themes ensure that your content conveys your brand's distinct voice and stance on essential topics, reinforcing your identity and values in every piece of communication.

CORE BRAND STORY

Your **Core Brand Story** (or **Brand Narrative**) is the overarching story that communicates your brand's identity, values, and purpose to your audience. It serves as the foundation for all brand communications—

both internal and external—and guides the selection and prioritization of your Story Pillars. The Core Brand Story ensures that all content aligns with your brand's mission and resonates consistently with your audience.

MESSAGING FRAMEWORK / MESSAGING MAP

A **messaging framework** is a structured approach to developing and delivering key messages that support your core brand story and business objectives. It considers your organizational goals and the needs of your target audience, outlining the core messages that internal teams use across various channels. The framework prioritizes different types of messaging, such as:

- Purpose Messaging
- Value Proposition Messaging
- Positioning Messaging
- Thought Leadership Messaging

This structured approach ensures coherence and effectiveness in all communication efforts. The Messaging Map we use at Forge & Spark is a way to document and create a reference for this framework.

CONTENT STRATEGY AND CONTENT MARKETING STRATEGY

Content Strategy encompasses the comprehensive planning, creation, delivery, and governance of all content across all channels, aligning with organizational goals and stakeholder needs. It considers the entire content lifecycle and a broad range of metrics to ensure content is compelling and aligned with overall business objectives.

Content Marketing Strategy is a subset of the broader content strategy, specifically focused on using content to attract, engage, persuade, and convert a target audience. Its primary objectives include driving marketing outcomes such as:

- Brand Awareness
- Community Building
- Lead Generation
- Customer Acquisition

A content marketing strategy involves identifying target audience personas, defining content themes, selecting distribution channels, and setting performance metrics to ensure content efforts are strategic and impactful.

STORYTELLING FRAMEWORK

A **storytelling framework** provides a structured approach to crafting compelling narratives that resonate with your audience. It typically includes elements such as:

- Character Development
- Plot Structure
- Conflict Resolution
- Emotional Engagement

This framework helps create memorable and impactful stories that communicate your brand's message and values.

CONTENT CALENDAR

A **content calendar** is a schedule that outlines the timing and frequency of content publication across various channels. It ensures that content is published consistently and aligned with critical events, seasons, or marketing campaigns. A well-maintained content calendar helps plan and organize content efforts, providing timely and relevant content delivery.

Cheat Sheet: How to Set Up and Use Your Messaging Map

To create your Messaging Map in Google Sheets or Excel, you can follow these detailed steps to help you structure your content. The Messaging Map typically has multiple sheets, each focusing on a specific aspect of your messaging strategy.

How to Create Your Map in Google Sheets or Excel

1. Open Google Sheets or Excel

- Open a new document in either Google Sheets or Excel.
- Name the document something descriptive, like "Messaging Map for [Your Brand/Project Name]."

2. Sheet 1: Content OKRs

- Name the first sheet something like "Content OKRs."
- Create Column Headings:

  o Column A: Objective

  ☐ Define what you want to achieve with your content marketing. Objectives are ambitious and qualitative.

  ☐ Example: *Increase brand awareness among eco-conscious consumers.*

  o Column B: Key Result 1

  ☐ This is the first measurable outcome that defines success for the objective.

  ☐ Example: *Achieve 10,000 social media mentions in Q4.*

  o Column C: Key Result 2

  ☐ A second measurable outcome for the same objective.

- Example: *Increase website traffic from organic search by 20%.*

  o Column D: Key Result 3

  - A third measurable result, if necessary.

  - Example: *Secure three guest articles in sustainability-focused online publications.*

  o Column E: Progress (% Complete)

  - Track progress towards each Key Result. This could be a manual update based on team inputs (e.g., 50% complete).

  - Example: 50%

  o Column F: Owner

  - Identify the team member responsible for overseeing the progress of each Objective or Key Result.

  - Example: *John Doe (SEO Specialist)*

  o Column G: Due Date

  - Assign deadlines for completing each Objective or Key Result.

  - Example: *December 31, 2024*

By following these steps, your Content OKRs sheet will allow you to set ambitious goals, track progress, and ensure accountability within your content marketing team.

3. Sheet 2: Persona-Based Messaging

This sheet focuses on defining the core messages for each audience persona.

- Create Column Headings:

  - ☐ **Column A: Persona or Segment**

    - Enter the name and description of your audience persona or segment.

    - Example: *Eco-friendly Emma—A young professional, ages 25-35, focused on sustainability and reducing her environmental impact.*

  - ☐ **Column B: Job to Be Done**

    - ☐ List the tasks, goals, or emotional outcomes this persona seeks to achieve through interacting with your content. You can include both functional tasks and emotional states.

    - ☐ Example: *Researching eco-friendly home products.*

  - ☐ **Column C: Pains**

    - ☐ Identify the challenges or frustrations (the "pain points") this audience faces related to your product or service and how your content can help alleviate these issues.

    - ☐ Example: *High costs of eco-friendly products, need for more trusted information.*

  - ☐ **Column D: Gains**

    - ☐ Define the benefits this persona will receive from your product/service and your content. Highlight how your content will help them achieve their goals or meet their needs.

☐ Example: *Save money on eco-friendly products through discounts and gain confidence in product choices.*

☐ **Column E: Know**

☐ What must your audience know to take the desired action? This could include product features, facts, or educational information.

☐ Example: *Understand the environmental impact of each product.*

☐ **Column F: Feel**

☐ Define how you want the audience to feel after interacting with your content. This can include emotional states such as trust, excitement, or urgency.

☐ Example: *Feel confident and reassured that their purchase supports sustainability.*

☐ **Column G: Believe**

☐ What belief must your audience hold about your brand or product to take action? This is the more profound conviction that leads to trust and engagement.

☐ Example: *Believe that your brand is genuinely committed to sustainability.*

☐ **Column H: Action**

☐ What action do you want your audience to take after consuming your content? This could be subscribing, purchasing, downloading, etc.

☐ Example: *Sign up for eco-friendly product updates.*

☐ **OPTIONAL Columns for Stage-Based Messaging**

  ☐ Are there specific messages you must assign to Top of Funnel, Mid Funnel, and Bottom of Funnel Messaging? Include them here if so.

  ☐ Examples: Check this out. Are you interested in learning more? / Buy now

☐ **OPTIONAL Columns for Content Ideas & Additional Messaging**

  ☐ Filling in this sheet will undoubtedly prompt ideas for specific content and additional messages you don't want to forget; I recommend including a column or two here to capture these as they arise.

4. Sheet 3 and Beyond (Optional)

You can add more sheets as needed to map other elements like:

- **Brand Messaging:** Focused on overarching messages like value propositions, mission, and vision statements.

- **Product/Service Messaging:** Messaging tailored to individual products or services.

- **Call-to-Action (CTA) Messaging:** Specific CTAs you want to use in marketing campaigns.

5. Formatting Tips:

- **Use Colors:** Apply different colours to highlight personas, key pain points, or messages to make the sheet easy to navigate.

- **Freeze Top Rows:** Freeze the top row with your headers so you can quickly scroll through data without losing track of columns.

- **Add Filters**: Use filters to sort and focus on specific personas or messaging details when needed.

- **Conditional Formatting**: Use conditional formatting to highlight important columns, such as "Pain Points" in red or "Core Message" in bold.

6. Save and Share

- Save your document in a cloud platform (Google Drive or OneDrive) so it's accessible to your team.

- Share access with key team members to collaborate on or review the messaging map.

Following these steps, you'll have a structured, interactive Messaging Map that provides clear guidance for content creation and marketing efforts tailored to your audience's needs.

ABOUT THE AUTHOR

Shannon Emmerson is a content strategist, agency leader, and founder of Forge & Spark Media, a Certified B Corp content marketing agency based in Vancouver, B.C. that's dedicated to helping purpose-driven brands connect, grow, and thrive.

With decades of experience in internal communications, publishing, and content marketing for brands big and small, Shannon knows how to craft messaging that builds trust and creates genuine connections. She's worked with everyone from local businesses to global organizations, blending strategic smarts, creative flair, and a deep belief in marketing as a force for good.

Shannon is a sought-after speaker and consultant who's passionate about helping leaders share their stories with purpose and impact. She loves nothing more than guiding purpose-driven brands to communicate authentically, inspire their audiences, and drive meaningful change.

ENDNOTES

1 https://www.edelman.com/news-awards/2023-edelman-trust-barometer

2 https://www.edelman.com/trust/2023/trust-barometer/special-report-trust-climate/brands-help-consumers-lead-meaningful-sustainable-lifestyle

3 https://www.trustsignals.com/blog/edelman-trust-havas-trust-studies

4 https://www.edelman.com/trust/2023/trust-barometer/special-report-trust-climate/brands-help-consumers-lead-meaningful-sustainable-lifestyle

5 https://migroup.com/blog/edelmans-2023-brand-trust-report-what-brands-and-agencies-need-to-know/

6 https://www.trustsignals.com/blog/edelman-trust-havas-trust-studies

7 https://www.statista.com/statistics/1179261/leading-corporations-reputation-united-states/

8 https://www.patagonia.com/actionworks/home/choose-location/

9 https://time.com/5052617/patagonia-ceo-suing-donald-trump/

10 https://www.outsideonline.com/outdoor-adventure/exploration-survival/patagonia-donates-1-million-georgia-voting-rights/

11 https://bettermarketing.pub/dont-buy-this-jacket-patagonia-s-daring-campaign-2b37e145046b

12 https://bettermarketing.pub/dont-buy-this-jacket-patagonia-s-daring-campaign-2b37e145046b

13 https://ca.linkedin.com/in/hannah-spackman-a8180086?trk=public_post-text

14 https://www.linkedin.com/posts/mountainequipmentcompany_liveyourpurpose-outdoorlife-epicadventures-activity-7211808482574958592-Y74j

15 https://resourcecenter.infinit-o.com/blog/10-zappos-stories-that-will-change-the-way-you-look-at-customer-service-forever/

16 https://en.wikipedia.org/wiki/Five_whys

17 https://www.kantar.com/Inspiration/Brands/The-Journey-Towards-Purpose-Led-Growth

18 https://forgeandspark.com/why-good-personas-matter-in-content-and-digital-marketing/

19 https://ir.allbirds.com/news-releases/news-release-details/allbirds-announces-promotions-within-its-executive-leadership

www.ingramcontent.com/pod-product-compliance
Lightning Source LLC
Chambersburg PA
CBHW040916210326
41597CB00030B/5094